# It all began in a Garden...

# Gulf Coast Gardening

## With

# Randy Lemmon

**Front and back cover photos by
Julie Nanni**

**www.photographictechniques.com**

## Published by

## Randy Lemmon Consulting

Published by Randy Lemmon Consulting

Publisher: Randy Lemmon

21102 Begonia Creek Ct.  Cypress, TX 77433

**www.randylemmon.com**

First Edition, printing  July 2005

Second Edition, printing  September 2006

This book is dedicated to Yvonne and Randal; my wife and son. Everything positive that happens in my life is because they came into my life.

# Table of Contents-

# Foreword-

Gardening is a learning process, which also happens to be part science and part art form. Randy Lemmon's book is able to combine the two in a way that turns this book into a resource that every first time homeowner along the Gulf Coast must have. Experienced gardeners should have it in their resource arsenal too.

My gardening experience comes from 35 years of running a 14 acre retail nursery and landscape business in Seabrook, Texas. It has been a privilege to associate ourselves with Randy and his GardenLine radio program. I've been impressed with how much Randy has learned in just 10 years of doing GardenLine, proving he "really knows his stuff."

I am a compulsive learner about all topics. I like to learn about history, math, science and yes, gardening. Over the years, I have traveled the world looking for interesting things to bring back to the nursery to sell. Learning about new cultures and bringing back cool things from other parts of the world is great fun, but the best part is learning.

I can see how much Randy likes to learn about this industry, inside and out. Then, to see much of what Randy talks about all year long on the radio, condensed into one easy to read rule book for Gulf Coast gardening. We are lucky that Randy would take the time to put this great information on paper for all gardeners to learn from.

Jim Maas

Maas Nursery

Seabrook, Texas

June 2, 2005

# INTRODUCTION

So, why should you buy this book?  That's usually the first question anyone ever asks when buying a self-help or how-to book.  Here's why I think this book will really help.

It's the ultimate RULE BOOK for Gulf Coast landscaping.   If you follow these rules you will have a beautiful landscape.

Many gardening books are chock-full of pretty pictures, but not filled with much practical how-to advice.   I could provide beautiful photos too, but I think you are better served if you have a complete understanding of all the concepts that make Gulf Coast landscapes work.  The GardenLine radio show is all about questions and answers and we are quite successful in that vein. A radio station co-worker, named Jennifer Huther, looked through the text before we went to print and said "This is like having a year's worth of your radio show condensed into one easy-to-read guide." That blew me away.  She was so right, because this book really is a compilation of all the advice I give out year after year answering people's individual garden questions.

I also think this book is going to be exceptionally helpful for anyone who is new to Gulf Coast gardening.  I make the joke on the radio show all the time to people, who move here from other northern and western states, that they have to forget everything they know about gardening and start over.  Maybe that concept can best be summed up in this email I received from a loyal listener, who is now succeeding with this kind of advice.

*Randy,*

*Thank you for saving my trees from the Crape Myrtle Massacre. We moved here 3 years ago, from Michigan, into a new home. At final inspection we were told, "Oh, you cut this to about 3 feet every year around February" So we moved in the end of February and I cut it.....then I started listening to you. 3 years later, look at the size of my gently pruned Crape Myrtle and the abundance of blooms!!! My only regret is that we didn't move it further from the house since it's getting so huge!*

*Thanks for my beautiful Crape Myrtle!*  **Debbie Johns**

# Chapter One-

# Building the Perfect Beds
*It's all about the soil*

# BUILDING THE PERFECT BEDS

Almost all gardening success in Texas and the Gulf Coast, be it vegetable gardening, general landscaping or even simple flowerbeds, begins with good soil. Unfortunately, in most of the Gulf Coast Region we don't have anything resembling good soil. In fact, most of it is pitiful. That's because the majority of our soil is clay-based. Some people call it CLAY, while others call it CALECHE or even GUMBO. And, of course, the closer you get to the coastline, the sandier the soil becomes. Whatever the case, it's simply not the best soil to plant in, unless it is amended.

Sadly, just adding some humus or compost to a hole you dig doesn't necessarily make it a worthwhile planting medium. That's why garden-advice blabbermouths (such as myself) are always emphasizing the importance of "building raised beds."

## YOU CAN'T GO WRONG WITH ROSE SOIL

When I'm talking about building a raised bed, I'm not talking about blending it to the existing soil. I'm stating that you must "build a raised bed" on top of existing soil.

In my last book, I mentioned Garden Mix quite a bit. And while that's still a viable option to use for basic landscaping purposes, it's Rose Soil that has really developed quite a reputation for Gulf Coast gardening.

Some 10 years ago, Rose Soil, by the bag or by the bulk, wasn't as readily available as it is today. Also, in the past five years, even more "blended" soils have come to the market, including Landscaper's Mix, Azalea Soil, Hill Country Soil and Tropical planting mixes.

So to make it simple, you can't go wrong with Rose Soil, Landscapers Soil or a Garden Mix, when buying it by the bag or bulk. Again, this is almost always needed for landscapes, vegetable gardens, flower beds and even potted plants.

# WHAT IS ROSE SOIL?

Rose Soil, to the gardening enthusiast, is the perfect blend of top soil, sand and humus; top soil gives it body, sand for drainage and humus is decomposing mulch-like material that will continuously help the soil become richer and more friable.

A typical raised bed, for landscaping purposes, needs to be at least 8 inches but no more than 12 inches above the existing soil profile. Yes, you can till Rose Soil into the existing soil for a few inches as well. However, that shouldn't stop you from making an additional 6-8 inches of a pure raised bed on top of that. Again, the goal is to achieve a "raised bed." You're not trying to make the clay soil instantly better.

Then it's important to "lock it in." You can do that any number of ways: Landscape stone, moss rock, ledgers, pre-cast bricks, landscape timbers, limestone, river rock, etc. Yes, you can use "edging" material, (You know, the 4-6 inch green or black plastic or sometimes metal strips?) but unless you're desperate, please avoid them. Not only do these antiquated landscaper edging materials look like something from 20 years ago, more often than not they come loose. Plus, metal ones inevitably rust.

It's a fact that you shouldn't build a raised bed right up next to the foundation of a house. Weep holes should never be blocked at the foundation, either by soils or mulches. (We will get into mulching details later in this book.) That's why I always recommend laying a few inches or up to two feet of river rock up next to the foundation. Then you can start your "raised bed" from that point. This serves three very important purposes: 1. You keep from covering up the weep holes. 2. You have access behind the landscaping, which helps when pruning or treating the bed 3. The most important benefit is how it keeps insects, namely ants and termites from having easy access to (and through) the weep holes.

It's also important to remember that a "raised landscape bed" doesn't need to be 8-10-12 inches throughout every part of the bed. It is important for it to be at its highest "raised" depth towards the center, where you plan on planting larger shrub elements. Raised beds can taper down both sides from the center and back to as little as four inches, if need be. And that's where you will add color elements like annuals or perennials, which only need a few inches to get started.

However, if you do build such a raised bed with such tapering, and don't "lock it in" as discussed earlier, you will eventually see it erode away over a period of time.

## SOIL FOR VEGETABLE GARDENS

Has someone asked the question about vegetable gardens and whether or not they can be successful with just Rose Soil or Garden Mix? It will work, but won't produce the greatest product. While a landscape bed can be the sand-soil-humus mix of a Rose Soil, a successful vegetable garden must have even more organic compost/humus.

I say the perfect blend for a vegetable garden is two parts Rose Soil and one part organic compost. Or seen another way, 1/3 of your soil needs to be really good compost. Everyone has a different opinion about what kind of compost is best. If you have your own compost pile, I hope it has been decomposing for 6 months. Most compost, already in bags, usually meet that standard. There are composts derived from mulches, cow manure, sheep manure and even specialty blends with turkey waste and rice hulls. Just make sure it's compost. Personally, I've had great success with well-composted cow manure by the bag. Again, everyone has his or her own philosophy about what works. So, ask someone you know who is successful at vegetable gardening what their recipe might be.

But one thing that is very true, and constant about vegetable gardening is that it truly needs to be raised a minimum of 10 inches. Most people I know that start a vegetable garden (and a rose garden) don't even try to kill the grass or weeds in the area they designate for their vegetable bed. All it takes to suppress the grass or weeds in that area is to lay down several layers of newspaper, probably 8-10 pages thick, and cover that up with the raised bed. Over time, the paper will breakdown and become part of the soil. In the meantime, it's preventing any kind of weed or grass from growing up through your pristine veggie garden.

## SOIL FOR FLOWER BEDS

As you may have noted earlier in this chapter, simple raised flower beds for seasonal color, may not need to be as deep as that for vegetable gardens or landscape elements. Since most annuals and even some perennials are purchased in containers that are four to six inches deep, and since their roots are likely to "spread out" as opposed to anchoring themselves downward, they can thrive in a four-to-six inch raised area.

Incidentally, don't apply this four to six inch raised bed rule around the base of trees. I realize many of you think (thanks mostly to ill-informed landscapers and the notorious model home effect) that you can plant flowers around the base of trees. If you follow my advice, and the advice of most tree experts along the Gulf Coast, you should never try to plant flowers and other landscape plants around the ring of trees. The only exception to that rule would involve permanent groundcovers, which don't need more than a couple of inches of growing medium. Keep in mind that so-called tree experts have insisted for years that you shouldn't bring in more than two inches of dirt/fill/sand per year to fill in areas around trees. More than that suffocates the root system of the tree. Mulch is the exception to that rule.

What if grass or weeds exist in the area where I want to build the raised bed? Well, if you don't plan on planting bigger landscape specimens like a five-gallon shrub, then follow the advice from the vegetable garden example and lay down newspaper. However, few if any people will plant only 1-gallon shrub specimens in the garden. Which is why it's important to either cut out the sod (and that's hard work) or kill the grass/weeds with a non-selective herbicide like Eraser®, Killzall®, Roundup® or Finale®. Those are all marketed names of glyphosate herbicides that kill any grass or weed. Once the grass is dead, it makes it that much easier to till out the dead material. Also, you get the added benefit of some loosened clay soil to start your "raised bed."

You may also be asking about how this soil discussion applies to trees and larger specimen shrubs? Well it doesn't. I have a method for planting trees and shrubs that works very well, but it is discussed in detail a bit later in our overall discussion of trees for the Gulf Coast.

I will make this warning: No matter how small the tree you want to transplant, it won't be a long-term success in a 10-inch raised bed because of the instability of the soil. A tree really needs to anchor its roots more firmly into the ground. Ironically, that's where some good clay-based soil does come in handy.

If you feel like you're in a quandary as to how much Rose Soil, etc. you will need to make the ultimate raised bed, here is a basic rule: Remember first that soil is measured by the CUBIC YARD. In order to raise your soil level by 4 inches, you will need to divide the square footage of the area you're working with by 73. That number will help determine the cubic yards needed. Then remember that you will need two times that amount for an 8 inch raised bed, and three times that amount for a 12-inch raised bed.

For example: My square footage for gardening in raised beds is 150 square feet. (5 feet wide by 30 feet long). Divide 150 by 73 and you've got about 2 cubic yards (What normally fits in the back of a large pickup) For an 8-inch raised bed you would need about 4 cubic yards and thus for a 12-inch raised bed 6 cubic yards.

Now that may sound like a lot of soil, but keep in mind that 150-square foot measurement is a big bed. If you're dealing with anything over 2 cubic yards of soil, you will need to go to a soil yard or have it delivered. Buying Rose Soil by the bag (with such requirements as written here) can get cost-prohibitive. It is always cheaper to buy mulches and soils in bulk.

## WHAT IF THE SOIL IS SANDY?

If you live more towards the Piney Woods or close to the coast, and you think your soil is sandy, you will need less sand in the Garden Mix/Rose Soil. Such mixes can be blended specifically for you at most soil yards. You may not need to build raised beds the farther north you go and the more woodsy it is; especially if there is plenty of forest floor debris.

Unfortunately, most typical quarter acre home sites aren't developed in areas with rich soils. Instead they are built upon piles of bank sand and clay. So, if you are fortunate to have a more forest floor-like base of soil, use it to your advantage.

## CAN I MAKE MY EXISTING BEDS "RAISED BEDS"

The answer to that is somewhat complicated. It doesn't deserve a simple YES or NO! Here are some basic tenets to keep in mind if you want to transform an existing bed to a truly raised bed.

The first and the most obvious answer is to extract all your existing smaller shrubs and landscape elements and start over using all the "building the perfect bed" rules discussed previously.

The second most often applied rule is to aerate the soil occasionally adding good mulches, soil foods and micronutrients, letting the soil get better with help over a long period of time. People can accomplish this simply by updating mulch levels twice a year and poking holes occasionally with something like metal rod. Then, spray soil activators or organic foods a few times a year.

The third idea, most commonly applied, is to leave the larger shrubs in place and build somewhat raised beds adjacent to them, to give the newer plants and flowers a better chance at success.

The last tenet, if applied to larger shrubs and trees that just aren't growing, is to "re-set" them. Re-set the shrubs in re-built beds and re-set the trees with the process discussed in detail on the Trees chapter of this book.


## SOIL FOR ACID-LOVING PLANTS


I mentioned very early in this chapter all the different soils available on the market today, by bag or in bulk. My second favorite soil for landscaping purposes is Azalea Soil. The same companies who have Gulf Coast ties and who make Rose Soil also make an Azalea Soil. In Houston, the Azalea Soil was developed specifically for a group that helps take care of the popular Azalea Trail.


The beauty of Azalea Soil is how perfect it is for what I call all the Yah-Yah plants (In deference to all my Greek friends out there, no, I do not mean "Yia Yia!"). Azaleas, gardenias, hydrangeas, camellias and magnolias are all well-known, acid-loving plants. I call them Yah-Yah plants because of the way all of their pronunciations end.


But since most of the aforementioned Yah-Yah plants need an acid soil consistently, you will still need to pay attention to the pH needs of such plants. Most of them thrive in a soil where the pH is 5.5 to 6.5, or somewhat acidic. However, Azalea Soil will not stay acidic naturally, so you will over time have to add acid and iron. Remember on a pH meter, 7.0 is neutral. Anything above that is considered alkaline.


Lastly, raised beds don't always stay "raised" for a long time, which is why adding mulch helps keep the beds organic and friable over time. There will be more on the mulches later. It's also fair game to add soil activators and micronutrients to raised beds from time to time. There are liquid versions like soil activators from Medina, plus hormones and vitamins in products like Super Thrive. The newest way to boost the soil from time to time is to use the granular or "pelletized" micronutrients also known as soil food. Heck, you can even sprinkle many of the newly formulated organic composts into a bed. They have been pressurized in such a way that you can broadcast many organic fertilizers with a simple hand-held broadcast spreader like you would a granular fertilizer.

# Chapter Two-

# Top Trees for the Gulf Coast
*The 15 best trees for shade purposes*

# TOP TREES FOR THE GULF COAST

In my first book, I noted that I received more questions about trees than almost any other subject. I have to admit that turf questions far outweigh the tree questions eight years later. Nevertheless, tree questions still run a close second.

The most obvious question I get has to be, "What is the fastest growing shade tree?" What hasn't changed from the first book is that there is no one "silver bullet" or "fool-proof" answer. That's because everyone has different requirements in terms of space and soil conditions. This is also why I keep revising what used to be my Top Ten List. It was a Top Dozen a few years ago, and has now grown to a Top 15 Trees for Houston and the Gulf Coast. Additionally, there are also a few Honorable Mentions along the way.

The Top 15 do have to meet certain requirements:

> **1. They have to be acclimated to the Gulf Coast climate -- I assume that would go without saying.**
>
> **2. Gives us the best chance at the shortest time for an ample shade tree.**
>
> **3. Something that is readily available at reputable nurseries and tree farms along the Gulf Coast.**

I have broken this down into two tiers: **The Top Seven –** These are the first choices you should make at all possible times. In almost every case, they grow fast, are adapted to our climate, and quite readily available. **The Second Eight** – These are what I refer to as secondary choices. That means they shouldn't be the only trees you have in the landscape but can supplement one or more from the Top Seven.

The beauty of the chapter in this book is that you take this book with you when going to a garden center, tree farm or nursery etc. (I suppose you could print it out if you ordered it online) in order to cross reference the actual botanical name along with the common name, so that you don't get something you weren't after. The perfect example of this would be if you are looking for a Green Ash (Fraxinus penssylvanica). My goal is that you don't pick up something that simply says Ash Tree. If you can't be genetically certain by the Latin name, then it is likely an Arizona Ash (Fraxinus velutina), which have a very limited life span along the Gulf Coast.

# THE TOP SEVEN

**1. LAUREL OAK -- (*Quercus laurifolia*)** -- This tree, simply put, has become my favorite tree for Gulf Coast landscapes. It can grow in almost any soil and grows so quickly to a shade tree that it's almost scary. Many people mistake it for a Willow Oak, but the Laurel Oak's leaves are a bit longer. Like the Willow Oak, the Laurel has that shiny leaf and compact growing habit. When I say "compact" I don't mean short tree growth. I mean a dense/compactness to the leaf growth. That's what makes it such an awesome shade tree. It can often be labeled as a Swamp Laurel Oak or a Darlington Oak. However, if you make certain that it says *Quercus laurifolia* on the tag, you can rest assured that this absolutely is the fastest-shade tree for the Gulf Coast.

> **PROS:** Can reach over 100 feet in height at maturity, but can reach 30 feet easily within the first 3 years. Has a shiny leaf, similar to certain Live Oaks. This tree grows so compact/so dense that it certainly will provide ample shade very soon. A true Laurel Oak, although deciduous by definition, does not shed all its leaves each winter. That's why it is often mistaken for an evergreen. And it always grows a tall, straight trunk. *Quercus laurifolia* is also considered a Texas Native species.

**CONS:** Considering its prodigious growth, it is not for small yards, for it will provide too much shade too quickly. If not trimmed/pruned properly, Laurels can get too dense and grow really tall rapidly without filling out properly.

## 2. GREEN ASH – (*Fraxinus penssylvanica*) -- Do you know the old saying "ASH IS TRASH"? Well, that only applies to the Arizona Ash, as noted above. I was told long ago that the Green Ash was the next best thing to an Arizona Ash, when it comes to fast growth. I've planted a few over the years, and have never been disappointed. I took a sapling Green Ash from a charity function in 1997 that was not quite 3 feet tall and simply a twig. That tree in 2005 is easily over 40 feet tall with a 20 foot spread providing perfect shade against the setting sun. I don't live in this house anymore, but I drove by it just the other day to confirm how big it had gotten.

**PROS**: Can top out at 50 or 60 feet. Will grow very fast but does not have the nasty seed pods that the Arizona Ash has. This tree is one of the last to lose its leaves in Fall/Winter.

**CONS**: You can often be fooled into buying an Arizona Ash versus the desired Green Ash if they are generically labeled "ASH" at the nursery. This is why it is always good to cross-reference the botanical name *Fraxinus penssylvanica*. It is also one of the last to push out new growth in early spring.

## 3. NUTTALL OAK – (*Quercus nattallii*) -- The leaves of the Nuttall are somewhat similar to the Shumard Red Oak and the Overcup Oak. (Both good trees, by the way) Once again make sure that you have the right Latin name when cross-referencing at a nursery or tree farm. Of those three trees (Nuttall, Shumard, and Overcup), I'm convinced that the Nuttall is the best. It too has excellent fall color but with more orange and yellow leaves as opposed to the red and purple of the

Shumard. The biggest difference is in the look of the acorn. The acorns are so unique in that they are much larger and have a special striped look as well. The Nutall is often found in more coastal nurseries as the Swamp Red Oak.

> **PROS:** Another tree that can easily reach over 60 feet at its maturity, which means fast growth. As noted, this tree has beautiful fall color, if temperatures cooperate, of distinctly yellow/orange/red autumn leaves. This tree is very well acclimated to clay soils. I like them so much I have two very nice sized ones in my landscape.

> **CONS:** This is one of the few trees with scant criticisms. The main negative I find is that it is often mistaken for a Shumard Red Oak. Which also translates into that it may not be as readily available.

**4. SHUMARD RED OAK – (*Quercus shumardii*)** -- Because it is often times more readily available than the preferred Nuttall, Shummard Red Oaks are becoming the most popular tree for landscape contractors. Again, a fast growing tree that can not only reach its 60 foot height at maturity rather quickly, it can get a 40 foot spread as well. The Shummard's popularity may be driven not just by its rapid growth, but more importantly, its beautiful fall colors of red and bronze. This tree is also tolerant of clay and highly alkaline soils. The best tip I've been able to give anyone when picking out a Shummard Red Oak is to pick them during the fall months to assure you're getting one that provides bright red leaves in the fall. Another bit of sound advice on the Shummard is to make certain that it is planted in an area with good drainage.

> **PROS:** Fast growth and wide span. This tree is more readily available than its closer cousins of Nuttall and Overcup. The Shummard holds its leaves longer than others during the winter, which gives it unique character.

**CONS:** Like others that hold on to leaves a bit longer in the fall and winter, the Shummard is one of the last to leaf out in the spring. Since it has a wide spread, it needs lots of room and often can't be planted within 20 feet of a foundation. Because it holds onto the brown versions of what used to be red/orange leaves well into the winter, many people think it looks dead.

**5. WHITE ASH --** *(Fraxinus Americana)* -- This is even faster growing than the Green Ash. That also means it can get tall quickly without getting as wide as we desire in a shade tree. But like the Green Ash, the White Ash is not as susceptible to the diseases and insect pressures that Arizona Ashes are. Quite often the White Ash is labeled as a Texas Ash in many coastal nurseries and tree farms. Again, just make sure you cross-reference the Latin name.

**PROS**: Like the Green Ash, it is longer-lived than the basic Arizona Ash. Often times this is more readily available than the Green Ash. It grows very tall, very fast. This Ash tree can actually develop striking fall color too.

**CONS:** Because it grows so tall so fast, it doesn't fill out for a wider spread like other trees in this list for the "dense" shade effect. It is often labeled as a Texas Ash in many coastal nurseries. Thus, it is not as readily available as the Green Ash.

**6. OVERCUP OAK –** *(Quercus lyrata)* -- It's sort of a shame that this is not that common of a tree in nurseries and garden centers. It has been gaining in popularity, but, still is not nearly as available as a Nuttall or a Shumard. Landscape professionals like Overcup because of its unique upswept branches that need very little pruning. While it is considered a fast grower, by Gulf Coast Gardening definitions, it will never be a very tall shade tree maxing out at 45 feet.

**PROS:** Fast growth. Upswept branches usually mean there is never a need for pruning. It is an extremely popular choice among innovative landscapers.

**CONS:** Will only reach 40-45 feet at maturity. Not as available through retail nurseries as Nuttall and Shummard.

**7. DRUMMOND RED MAPLE – (*Acer rubrum*) --** If anyone moves to the Gulf Coast from anywhere up north, they always want to plant Maples. Unfortunately, we have only a couple of maple varieties that can succeed along the coast. Thankfully, one of them is the Drummond Red Maple – a.k.a. The Scarlet Maple and Swamp Maple. By its name, you would think that everyone likes it because of its red color in the fall. But, it's the unique red leaves that emerge in early spring that really make the tree special to me. This tree can reach 70 feet at maturity, and can establish in some of the poorer soils of the Gulf Coast. But, please, be forewarned, that many nurseries try to sneak a Silver Leaf Maple in under the name of the Drummond. A Silver Leaf Maple is one of only three trees I would never plant along the Gulf Coast.

**PROS**: Very fast growth and wide spread. Unique colors on emerging leaves in spring. The hardiest of maple trees for the Gulf Coast.

**CONS**: Fall color development is not always reliable in Texas' autumn conditions. Unfortunately, lazy and/or ignorant nurseries will generically label Silver Leaf Maples as Drummond in order to make a sale.

## THE SECOND EIGHT

1. **Mexican Sycamore – *(Plantanus mexicanus*)** -- Pros: Very fast growth that can often reach 100 feet or more at maturity. Very unique silver underside of leaves, so, if you wanted a Silver Leaf Maple, this is a much better

alternative. Isn't as susceptible to anthracnose like other Sycamore trees. Cons: Can almost grow too fast like other Sycamores, setting itself up for early decline. The leaves can be an overwhelming mess in the fall and winter because they are big Sycamore-style leaves.

2. **Monterrey Oak -- (*Quercus polymorphus*)** -- a.k.a. Mexican Oak; Pros: Unique leaf color not only in fall but in spring when emerging too. One of the first to leaf out in spring. In more southern parts of Texas, the Monterrey won't lose its leaves like other deciduous trees in the fall and winter. Cons: Questionable hardiness if temperatures get into single digits. Not as fast growing as most of the others, unless planted in optimum medium. Not as readily available as it was 10 years ago.

3. **White Oak – (*Quercus alba*)** -- Pros: Can be a huge tree with some 30-year-old White Oaks known to be 100 feet tall with an equally impressive span of 60-70 feet. Many landscapers like this better than Live Oaks. It is actually prized as wood for furniture. Cons: Not known as the fastest growing of all the aforementioned oaks. Must be planted all by itself because of its potential size.

4. **Camphor -- *(Cinnamomum camphora)*,** a.k.a. the Camphor Laurel; Pros: This is a beautiful stately tree if freeze damage can be prevented. (More on that in a moment) It is one of the most aromatic trees available. The berries attract lots of wildlife. If it doesn't suffer from harsh freezes, it is mainly an evergreen tree for the Gulf Coast. Cons: Probably the "least" readily available of all the trees mentioned in this book. Can freeze back quite a bit during cold spells where low temperatures are in the single digits.

5. **Cedar Elm – (*Ulmus crassifolia*)** Pros: This is an incredibly tough tree for coastal areas. It does have the potential to grow to 75 feet at maturity, but, that is certainly at a slower pace than most of the Top Seven. However, this is a native Texas tree that many people cannot go wrong with because it actually tolerates many of our inherent stresses: alkaline soils, clay soils, too

much salt, urban pollution, drought stress, etc. Cons: This doesn't produce vast amounts of leaves, in a dense fashion; not the best shade tree. This tree is often not labeled correctly.

6. **Corky Winged Elm – (*Imus alata*)** a.k.a. Winged Elm; Pros: While this has very typical elm-like leaves, it has very unusual bark. Some twigs have a twisted, cork-like look to them. The bark on the tree also has a twisted cork-like look.

7. **Bur Oak - (*Quercus macrocarpa*)** – The Bur Oak also has many other names by which it is known. a.k.a. Mossycup Oak and Prairie Oak. Pros: While this tree is probably better served farther north of the coastal regions, it still can grow to a majestically tall tree and is extremely drought tolerant. Bur Oaks are noted for their very large leaves and acorns. Cons: It's those long leaves and big acorns that most people don't like, making it hard to rake them in the fall. The acorns, which can be as big as two inches, are painful to step on too. It has a long taproot which makes it hard to transplant, even when very small

8. **Water Oak – (*Quercus nigra*)** The Water Oak may easily be the most often-used tree by landscapers, because it is usually the cheapest in price. Water Oaks are often mislabeled or known as many other names such as Possum Oak, Spotted Oak and Punk Oak. (Who you calling a PUNK?) It is also often misnamed as Post Oak. As noted in its name, the Water Oak can survive in oxygen-depleted soils along river banks. This is why it survives in so many stressed areas in Texas. Cons: It can often grow too tall, too fast, making a spindly form and the result is a weak tree that can come out of the ground during high winds.

## Honorable Mentions

These are trees that have more problems than they are worth in the long run, but they are readily available at tree farms and nurseries.

**Live Oak – *(Quercus virginiana*)** – Notoriously slow grower, that has to be pruned professionally and quite consistently to get the best results. However, the canopy or spread of a Live Oak at maturity can often be twice as wide as it is tall. There are hundreds of true different varieties of Live Oaks. That's just one of many reasons why it's so hard to make specific Live Oak recommendations. Unfortunately, garden advice givers, such as yours truly, always lump them as one. Yet, if you can find the Q. *virginiana,* then you're likely to get the variety that is adaptable to almost any soil condition along the Gulf Coast – with the exception of extremely sandy soil.

**Bradford Pear/ Aristocratic Pear – *(Pyrus calleryanna*)** -- The biggest downside with Bradford Pears is how they suffer from fire blight. It doesn't necessarily kill the tree but can make it very unsightly at times. The true Bradford has a unique wine glass shape. While other pears in the group, like the Callery and Aristocratic, don't have the same upward curve of the limbs as does the Bradford. But the Callery and the Aristocratic don't suffer from fire blight as much either. When planted close together, Bradfords make a stunning entrance or visual block up and down driveways and roadsides. When grown together in such a row, they also make for great shade.

**Chinese Pistache – *(Pistacia chinensis)*** – This tree has some very unique fall foliage and is what it is most prized. But it is also extremely drought resistant, tolerant of almost any soil conditions, and highly pest resistant. It only gets to 35-40 feet tall at maturity. While most of the other trees are great shade trees for two story houses, this can eventually be a great shade tree for any one story building at such maturity. It's interesting to note, however, that while the fall foliage is beautiful with a myriad of yellow/orange/red/green, it is probably the last of all the aforementioned trees to flush with leaves in spring. For me, the Chinese Pistachio (as it is commonly referred to) is more a unique landscape element than a shade tree.

## Three Trees I Would Never Plant

1. Silver Leaf Maple -- (*Acer saccharinum*) – The sad part about this tree is that it grows so darn fast that it makes it tempting to plant it as a shade tree. It can grow 30 feet in the first three to four years. But, along the Gulf Coast, the Silver Maple is so riddled with insects and diseases – because of our heat and humidity – that it often has an extremely limited life span of 10 years of less. As noted, they are susceptible to many insects and diseases including Verticilliumn wilt and other canker diseases. Because it can grow so fast, that usually means weaker wood. Thus, the brittle wood and poor branch development result in severe breakage during ice and wind storms. As for insects, you name it, the Silver Leaf Maple can get them. Aphids, lacebugs and scale are the top three insects which can literally suck the life from a Silver Leaf Maple. Plus, because the wood is so weak, it is an open invitation to a number of borer insects on the trunk. Bottom line: This is probably the worst tree possible for Gulf Coast landscapes.

2. Pine Tree - I realize you may see a lot of pine trees, looking healthy, throughout the region. I have lots of respect for many of the native pine tree stands. But, as an added element to an existing landscape, there are so many other better choices. You see Pine trees added to suburban landscapes, but, when was the last time you saw one look good in the first 7 years? They struggle in the clay soils for many reasons. The first of which is that a pine tree has a tap root that is often as long as the tree is tall, but, when it is harvested from a tree farm for a new landscape, they often severe the taproot. That leads to an additional stress for the pine tree making them highly susceptible to insect pressures, the least of which is the pine bark beetle. I will give minor exception on the use of pine trees in the landscape if they are pot-grown. Also, if you use the

pine trees in far-away spots in the landscape where they are likely never to be a threat to the foundation of the house, you have tacit approval to use them. Still, you have to keep in mind that it can be over 15 years before a sapling grown from a container will ever be the kind of shade providing landscape tree we all strive to have. Their root systems are prone to come to the surface quicker than any other tree I know in search of moisture. Thus, if you don't deep root feed and water these trees consistently, their root systems will threaten sidewalks, driveways and in some cases, house foundations.

3. Hybrid Poplars – In almost all cases, the only reason anyone buys a Hybrid Poplar is because of advertising in Sunday supplement magazines. They totally romance the idea that you can have a tree that grows 10 feet per year. That may be true, that it grows tall and fast, but in almost every case it simply is a stick. There's never any canopy or spread on the branches and leaves. Keep in mind that our climatic differences also have a huge impact on how a Poplar thrives and survives. They are usually propagated and successfully incorporated into landscapes in California where heat and humidity are scarce. I'll tell you more of my opinions on Sunday supplement advertising later in this book, but for now, you should avoid any tree advertised in such supplement magazines.

# PLANTING TREES

For every tree suggested in this gardening guide, the true secret to success is in how they are planted. In other words, successful root develop is the ultimate way to have a successful shade tree establish in your landscape. Most people, who aren't educated to the gardening foibles along the Gulf Coast, usually dig a hole the size of the root ball of their new tree and slide the tree into the hole. With our preponderance of clay, that is something of a prison sentence to the root ball of that tree.

I have a technique I call "Twice As Wide & Half Again As Deep". If you follow this technique, you are doing everything you can to ensure that the root systems of a newly planted tree have some room in which to establish themselves. Many people have found, just digging a hole and popping in a tree's root ball doesn't always work. That's because, in most cases, the hole is dug just big enough for the root ball. Consequently, the roots are immediately faced with the need to penetrate the hard clay soil. So, the tree stagnates and doesn't seem to grow much at all. That's why I call it a prison sentence as opposed to a death sentence. By the way, this technique that we use for trees also works for large shrubs as well.

While most landscape plants should be planted in raised beds, trees will actually do just fine in "existing soil" if we just give them a helping hand. Some folks dig more accommodating large holes, but, they backfill with peet, humus, mulch or even fluffy potting soil mixes. That normally leads to an area that's continually too wet, so, the root system can't breath and the tree yellows and dies.

So, the tree planting maxim I've tried to live by is to help the tree properly adjust to the existing soil conditions. Since clay isn't really a very good environment, we have to add a permanent soil amendment. There are a few examples of soil amendments listed a bit later.

Here's where the "Twice As Wide & Half Again As Deep" technique comes into play. First, dig a hole two to three times wider than the root ball, and half-again the depth of the actual root ball. For example, if the container is 10 inches across and 10 inches deep, you will need a hole 20-30 inches across and 15 inches deep. When you dig the dirt out of the hole, throw the dirt on a drop cloth or tarp as you dig.

Next, add the permanent soil amendment to the dirt you've dug out. Every amendment has different dirt-to-amendment ratios, but you're almost always safe at 6-to-1 or 5-to-1 dirt-to-amendment.

Add enough of this mixture to the bottom of the hole so that when the tree is inserted, the top of the root ball is at ground level or even just ever so slightly raised, so that it's 1-inch above the soil line. You will need to tamp down the mixture in that "half-again" as deep part so that there won't be any air pockets. Then, center the tree in the hole, and fill in around the ball, tamping down continuously as you go. Don't worry about "compacting" the area ... the permanent soil amendment you've added will essentially keep the soil aerated.

Finally, build a mulch ring on top, and water in. In fact, water once a week for the first year of the tree's life.

As the tree's roots acclimate to their new environment, they'll strengthen enough to penetrate the harder clay soil beyond the zone you established. Again, the whole intention is to give the tree a head start towards acclimating to existing soil conditions.  Thus, if we can make the first year or two easier on the roots with the looser soil/amendment mixture, then the easier it is for the healthier roots to penetrate the hard clay soil when it reaches it again.

## *PERMANENT SOIL AMENDMENTS
Commercial Names

☐ Tru-Gro (kiln-fired rocks, a concrete byproduct)

☐ Schultz Soil Conditioner

☐ Fertilome Natural Guard Soil Conditioner (used to be known as Revive)

Non-Commercial (homemade) Alternatives

☐ Small pea gravel (the smallest you can find)

☐ Pure clay kitty litter

☐ Granular gypsum (pelletized gypsum)

☐ Haydite (crushed granite)


# DEEP ROOT FEEDING OF TREES


In our clay soils, tree roots are often in search of moisture and nutrients nearer to the soil surface when they detect nothing down deep where they prefer to be.  That's when roots start appearing near the surface, buckling sidewalks, and causing mower-mayhem all over lawns.  At least once every hour on GardenLine, I probably hammer home the importance of deep-root watering and feeding trees.


Listeners call because their trees haven't grown much since they planted them two years ago. Or they call about the roots of older trees coming out of the ground. These are examples of trees in dire need of deep-root watering and feeding.  The key is in developing holes in the earth above the root system that go down 18 inches. They can be developed with a Ross Root Feeder, a soil auger, a post-hole digger, or a tool you've designed yourself using something like a piece of steel rebar.

The bigger the holes, the fewer you will need. With smaller holes, like those made with tools like the Ross Root Feeder, the more you will need. If the holes are bigger than an inch in diameter, however, you will need to fill them with pea gravel or organic matter like mulch or compost. Smaller holes, Mother Nature fills gradually and naturally.

With the holes in place, nature and your watering system will provide plenty of moisture to trickle down the holes. However, I do recommend organic foods from time to time, to aid in the natural microbial breakdown. You don't have to water each individual hole. The same holds true for feeding, but if your holes are two inches in diameter or more (like post-hole size), you can soak those areas individually with organic foods or soil activators. With small holes, soak the entire area with a spray-on organic liquid. Or, use compost over the surface to slowly work its way down. I truly mean this: ANY ORGANIC FOOD WILL DO when feeding trees. To me, as long as it says "organic" I don't care whether it's liquid or granular in form.

## ADDITIONAL TIPS:

☐ Remember that your holes need to be both inside and outside the drip line. Start them at least two feet from the trunk of the tree.

☐ Remember how tree roots grow. Often, we picture them growing only laterally, but they will actually grow *down* in well-watered, organic soils.

☐ Remember that this process must be consistent. Even healthy mature trees will benefit from deep-root watering and feeding.

## WORDS OF WARNING:

☐ Just feeding with granular synthetic food actually eats up beneficial microbes that we want to increase down in the root zone. That's why I emphasize using organic foods for the roots of trees. Yes, you will get some green up with synthetic tree foods, but your overall goal should be healthier soils.

☐ If you're auguring with a drill bit bigger than two inches, it's wise to have gas, phone and other utility lines marked prior to drilling.

☐ Don't forget to add additional holes outside the "drip line" as the tree matures.

☐ Hire a tree service company if you think this is too much work.

# A Visual for Deep Root Feeding

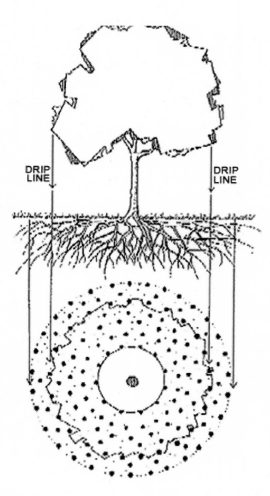

# Chapter Three-

## Landscape Shrubs
## for the Gulf Coast

*- Color-Tiering with Landscape Shrubs*
*- Randy's Top 30 Landscape Elements*

Writing a chapter on SHRUBS for the Gulf Coast was somewhat difficult. There probably needs to be a whole book dedicated to every shrub that could possibly work in Gulf Coast landscapes. Unfortunately for you, I'm too lazy and don't want to do that kind of research. Or, fortunately for you, I've simplified it. That way, you won't try things that don't work in this climate or that are riddled with insects and diseases.

Another vexing element that reared its head when writing this chapter was whether to stay true to the definition of a shrub. Should we allow for hardy perennials, certain tropicals, and larger growing bulbs? Again, if we are to take all those things into consideration, this could be a huge chapter.

It might even be an easier chapter to write if I just suggest Texas Natives for the vast majority of Texans who will read this book. That would allow me to eliminate a host of shrubs that might have semi-difficult care requirements.

So, where does that put us? As for me, I'm on the fence, getting splinters on my backside. I've never been one to follow rules very rigidly. I will definitely give you my best research for the Top 30 Shrubs that I think will work in almost any landscape along the Gulf Coast. I will also break down what I consider to be the best technique for giving instant character to a landscape called Color-Tiering. In another book I wrote, in the chapter about low-maintenance shrubs, I simply listed my top 20 favorite shrubs. But the list of top shrubs has grown to 30 in the past eight years. Furthermore, my experience with Color-Tiering has taught me that there is no better system for landscaping along the Gulf Coast.

I like to put this Color-Tiering into some perspective. You see, 30 years ago, when most people purchased a new home, landscaping was an afterthought. When folks in the suburbs did get around to landscaping, it seemed that ligustrums, junipers, pittisporums, or red tip photinias were the overwhelming choice. Not to mention, they were the only things in the landscape, as they were devoid of color and tropicals. Back then, a simple row of shrubbery was planted on each side of the front door, creating what I affectionately refer to as a "landscape-mustache."

Today, Gulf Coast landscapes have much more shape and depth to them. And with that depth is the need for different levels of landscape shrubs—different levels of both color and size. But instead of a hodge-podge of evergreens, I believe more people should try my color-tiering system. It can be done with two or three tiers. Anything more than three is difficult to maintain on a consistent basis.

You see, outside of adding color such as annuals and tropicals, most people don't think about adding color in the garden via the landscape shrubs. For me, "color-tiering" is all about the evergreen shrubs (with a few perennial exceptions). If the tiers are done correctly, you can actually set up a landscape plan with evergreens that can reduce long-term costs by reducing the need for copious flats of color. The trick is in picking the right plants for each tier with some kind of definitive contrast to each other's green leaves. The reason the color choice of the evergreen leaves is so important is because of the subtle differences in "green." A great example of this subtlety, and a bad choice, would be **Japanese Boxwoods** for the front and **Ligustrums** for the back. They both have a yellow hue to the evergreen leaves – thus, no color differential.

The second key to "color-tiering" your landscape shrubs would be choosing the appropriate size for each tier, especially when building a three-tier system. A two-tier system has a lot more room for error. Obviously, in both cases, the larger plants at maturity need to be in the back of the tiers. Those that can be maintained at a medium-height with consistent pruning should be in the middle tier. The dwarf versions and ground cover materials of others would be the front or lowest tier.

To me the front tier of a three-tier system in "color-tiering," is the toughest, and often times the most limited in selection. That is why in some instances, using perennials such as Mexican Heather is a viable option.

So without further ado, I give you three lists of plants that are mostly "evergreen" and that can be picked from to achieve a "color-tiering" landscape. You might notice that some are listed in two of the three categories, which is important if you choose two tiers over three. I'm sure you may have some of your own suggestions. In the meantime, here's a great starting point for those true do-it-yourselfers out there that want to achieve an elegant landscape without having to spend a ton of money – either on a landscaper or on huge sums of annuals each year. By the way, not many landscapers talk about "color-tiering" like I do. So, keep that in mind, if you decide to take these ideas to a landscaper and they roll their eyes at you. You'll also notice that I did not include what I refer to as the YAH-YAH plants – azalea, gardenia, hydrangea and camellia – because I'm a firm believer that they need to be in an acid-rich environment by themselves or with annuals and perennials that are "like feeders." One last warning: Some of these plants like full sun, some like full shade, and others can handle filtered light. It's incumbent upon you to determine which ones apply for your light requirements.

## BACK TIER/ANCHOR PLANTS/THE BIG ONES

Texas Wax Myrtle

Coppertone Loquats

Viburnum

Needlepoint Holly

Yaupon

Elaeagnus

Cleyera (for shadier environments)

Japanese Yew (for shadier environments)

Texas Sage (depending on ultimately shorter tier in front)

# MIDDLE TIER/MEDIUM SIZE PLANTS

Lorapetalum

Nandina (Compacta only)

Dwarf Burford Holly

Brunfelsia (aka – Yesterday, Today & Tomorrow)

Dwarf Yaupon

Plumbago

Gardenia

Texas Sage

Cleyera

Privet

Agapanthus (Lily of the Nile)

Wheeler's Pittisporums (for a 2-tier system)

Japanese Boxwood (for a 2-tier system)

Dwarf Yaupon

Dwarf Wax Myrtle


Mexican Heather (a perennial; also a groundcover/front tier in 3-tier system)

## FRONT TIER/LOWER PROFILE/SOMETIMES GROUNDCOVER

Aztec Grass (much hardier than variegated Liriope)

Liriope

Monkey Grass

Dwarf Monkey Grass

Katy Ruellia

Bulbine

Japanese Boxwood

Dwarf Yaupon

Dwarf Nandina

Ferns (Foxtail & Asparagus Ferns especially)

Wheeler Pittisporums

Mexican Heather/Cuphea

Groundcover Junipers

I bet many of you may already be asking questions about other plants that I always highly recommend, but are not in the color-tiering lists. Remember, this is a specific technique that mostly requires evergreen plants or perennials that don't lose their leaves in winter. As an example, even though I love ornamental grasses (such as purple fountain grass, lemongrass and muhly grass) they don't work in the color-tiering system because they go dormant for a long period in winter. Then there are plants like sago palms and dwarf pygmy date palms, which I love for a landscape, too, but need to be stand-alones or work as a corner accent. That is why they don't work for the color-tiering system in most cases.

## RANDY'S TOP 30 SHRUBS

Although this chapter will ultimately suggest a number of easy-to-care-for shrubs and while some of them will definitely fall into the "natives" category, most of them need some distinct TLC when they are first planted. A plant may be listed as "water-efficient" in some book or garden guide, however, that really isn't until after an "establishment period" will they require minimal water from the hose or irrigation system. So, no matter what you choose to plant in your landscape, consistent watering for the first two to three months is critical.

Another thing to consider towards long-term success and plant satisfaction is based largely on how well you prepare the raised beds/soils – if you'll recall the previous chapter on that subject.

Color-tiering and native plants aside, everyone in the gardening or landscaping business has their favorite plants. I am no exception. I'm going to give you my Top 30 List. By no means is this the "only" list, the "best" list or the most "comprehensive" list. This is MY LIST. It's simply ones I've worked with over the years that have either offered the lowest maintenance or the best adaptability. In this list are pearls that the average gardener can't, under normal conditions, mess up.

**Texas Wax Myrtle** (*Myrica cerifera*) -- a.k.a. Southern Wax Myrtle. Anyone who has listened to my radio show for any length of time, could probably tell you that the Wax Myrtle is hands-down my favorite landscape shrub. Ironically, most books on Texas gardening list it as a tree. I think it's the best damn shrub we can ever plant in our landscapes. It grows fast and stays green year round. It works in sun or filtered light and is tolerant of almost any soil condition. This is a true Texas native that is also very aromatic. It overcomes any problem it tends to encounter without any need for chemical assistance. There are also dwarf wax myrtles that are perfect for smaller landscapes. This shrub can get as high as 15 feet, but when trimmed consistently makes one of the best fence-line hedges for Gulf Coast landscapes. It can also get 10-12 feet wide.

**Lorapetalum** (*Chinese rubrum*) a.k.a. the Chinese fringe flower or fringe flower – There are many different varieties of lorapetalum available, please be very careful in your choice. I'm confident that anything with Fringe Flower on the label will be the kind you need, but I also suggest you avoid those that say "Razzleberri". Two things I love about the lorapetalum: 1.) They have distinctly maroon-ish, purple-ish to bronze leaves. 2.) They have striking fuschia-colored (almost Day-Glo pink) flowers two times a year. Based on the color-tiering system above, this is a perfect choice in almost every instance for the middle or medium-tier choice. This plant seems to do well in either sunny or even filtered light locations. It does not like to have wet feet, however, and can get over-watered to death. Best tip: feed it azalea food from time to time, if you want to darken up the leaves. Because of its versatility and popularity, this is also a variety of plant that keeps getting improved with new hybrid forms every few years.

**Sago Palm** (*Cycas revoluta*) – This is the first plant to break the rule of not being a "true" shrub. Heck, it's not even a true palm. It's actually from the Cycad family of plants that have been around since before the dinosaurs. However, because it works so well as a corner or "accent" piece to a landscape, it provides a remarkable look. This plant can also thrive in full sun or filtered light. Total shade is questionable for the sago palm. I've seen it do okay in the shade, in some instances, but they seem to mostly struggle. The seeds are poisonous to small dogs, if they eat one. So, harvest out the seeds from the center cones whenever possible.

**Agapanthus** (*Agapanthus orientalis*) a.k.a. Lily of the Nile. (Here we go breaking the "true" shrub rule again.) This is a bulb that simply does wonderful things as a landscape plant. Plus, you get the most magnificent blue globe-shaped bloom heads in May and June. But like most lilies, even when not in bloom, the agapanthus provides year round tropical looking green foliage as a nice alternative in any landscape. That is why I consider it a good landscape plant, if not a true shrub. Tell me where you've heard this before -- Lily of the Nile also works in sunny or some filtered light situations. But, it does need good drainage to thrive and survive.

**Duranta** (*Duranta repens*) a.k.a. Golden Dewdrop -- This plant/shrub/vine (whatever you want to call it) does not get enough play in our landscapes. I think it's not as popular as it could be because it is often mis-labeled. Yet, because it's so easy to care for more people should try it. This is a relaxed-look, slightly arching branches shrub that will max out at 7-8 feet in height, with gorgeous soft blue blooms. It's supposed to be tender in colder climates, but I just haven't seen it wither away since the 1989 freeze, so it is my opinion that the duranta has adapted to cooler weather. While some gardening books say it only blooms in May, I've seen blooms on some durantas from April through September. By the way, the golden dewdrop nickname comes from the fact it produces colorful yellow berries from time to time.

**Dwarf "Wheeler" Pittosporums** (*Pittosporum nana*) – Let's make a couple of things very clear. Yes, I hate regular pittosporums. I don't care much for the variegated ones either. I dislike them so much, I've nicked named them pitiful-sporums. But I can't stop loving what we call the Wheeler pittosporum. This dwarf variety of pittosporum will never grow any taller or any wider than 3 feet. This is another one of those multi-tasking plants that can do equally well in full sun or partial shade. The two unique things I love about Wheeler pitts: 1.) They are such a different color of green with a unique yellow hue to it. 2.) They make a great option for middle tiers and even front tiers in some color-tiering landscapes because of its unique color. If there is one down side to the Wheeler, it is that it can be nipped by freezing weather. These also have a great gardenia-like aroma for a month in early spring when flowering.

**Cleyera Japonica** (*Ternstroemia gymnanthera*) - This is the ultimate shrub for shade. There aren't many shrubs that can thrive in shady environments ( as opposed to the various groundcovers that can), however, this is the answer to many people's shady plant prayers. Cleyera is also good for filtered light situations, too. This plant has unique glossy leaves and a wonderful reddish bronze hue to the new growth. Most people keep Cleyeras pruned to 5 to 6 feet, but it can get as tall as 12 feet if left alone. It is a slow grower so it doesn't need pruning all that often. This is one of the hardiest plants for the Gulf Coast.

**Coppertone Loquat** (*Eriobotrya Coppertone*) – If you like photinias but hate the diseases, this is often a better alternative. It can still get fungal leaf spot diseases and some insects like scale, but not to the extent of red tip photinias, hollies and ligustrums. At full maturity this plant can get to 8 feet tall and 6 to 8 feet wide. It gets its coppertone name for the unique copper-colored new leaves.

**Oleander** (*Nerium Oleander*) – If you have small children and animals that will put anything and everything in their mouths, these are very poisonous plants, and probably shouldn't be in your landscape. But, it's hard not to recommend oleanders for Gulf Coast landscapes. So many colors are available these days, but the standards are hard to beat in red, white and pink. They don't need pruning every year, but should be pruned in October for best bloom production the next year. They can also become super drought tolerant if you can start cutting back gradually on watering in August. I've become an even bigger fan of the dwarf varieties and their unique colors like tangerine and yellow. Most research shows that they mature at 10 feet, but I've seen many oleanders eclipse 15 feet if left alone for years. However, the pruning keeps them fuller and more productive with blooms.

**Elaeagnus** (*Elaeagnus pungens*) – This is one of the more unique and extremely productive shrubs for the Gulf Coast landscape. The uniqueness of the elaeagnus comes with the leaves -- silver on the top and brownish bronze on the bottom. They also make a good security hedge because they are so thorny, yet, their uniqueness doesn't end there. They are one of the more prolific growers, but in a rather sporadic way. It's not the entire shrub that grows three feet each year, instead it's more like a few branches. This also leads to one of the downsides in that it has to be pruned quite a bit or it will look scraggly. Research says that it's supposed to grow to 8 feet tall at maturity, but I've seen that scraggly growth get much higher than that.

**Blue Plumbago** (*Plumbago auriculata*) – By definition, this is not a shrub. Instead it is defined as a perennial flower. The beautiful pale blue flowers are its best attribute. This plant is tender to freezing weather, and must be protected, but it always seems to bounce back even after a rough winter. In areas where it is protected from winter winds, it roars back with blooms from February through May. If fed blooming plant food throughout the summer, plumbago can still put out blooms for several months. I like it as a contrasting shrub in the landscape to all the green plants because it wants to produce those blue blooms for several months out of the year. While the plumbago is technically a perennial by horticultural standards, it can reach 4 to 5 feet at maturity, which is why I like it as a landscape shrub.

**Hibiscus** (*Hibiscus rosa-sinensis*) – Name a color and there's probably a version of the hibiscus that blooms in that hue. Red, white, pink, orange and yellow are the basics. But you can find many hybridized versions of hibiscus that blend all these colors and then some. By definition, this is a true tropical and by no means should be considered a permanent landscape shrub. However, if you are lucky enough to keep them from freezing, hibiscus will stay healthy and produce flowers year-round. Avoid using high phosphorous (bloom booster) fertilizers for hibiscus. They perform better with fertilizer ratios that are higher in nitrogen and potassium such as a 15-5-15. There are numerous hibiscus fertilizers on the market; just make sure the middle number isn't higher than the other two.

**Japanese Yew** (*Podocarpus macrophylla*) -- This is another of those great all-purpose plants depending on the light conditions. It can perform as well in full sun as it does in filtered shade. If trained correctly, yews grow in a columnar fashion or as an upright plant. By far, this is probably the easiest shrub to ever "prune to shape." And in shadier environments this plant is perfect as the anchor of the color-tiering system because it has such dark green leaves. You can also plant them on 3-foot centers to create a screen shrub over fence lines.

**Nandina** (Compacta & Dwarf mostly) I remember polling a number of landscapers 10 years ago to come up with a list of "favorite" shrubs. One landscaper wrote me back saying, "avoid nandinas in all cases." He's no longer in business. As long as you stick to the smaller and dwarf versions, you should never have a problem. The larger versions, often called heavenly bamboo, can spread vigorously if not constantly pruned and maintained. However, in all cases of Nandina, you get a very unique plant that bears a multitude of colors in the leaves alone. The normally delicate foliage turns brilliant shades of red, orange, maroon and yellow in the fall and winter. Then a bounty of red berries follows. This is one of those plants that they keep improving with new hybrids every couple of years.

**Needlepoint Holly** (*Ilex cornuta*) -- The Needlepoint Holly has a broad growth habit reaching 10 feet tall and 12 feet wide. *Ilex cornuta* 'Needlepoint' is very similar in looks to the dwarf Burford holly except it has a more upright growth habit and it is slightly taller when fully mature. It also has glossy dark green leaves with a small point on end and produces masses of dark red berries

**Indian Hawthorn** (*Raphiolepis indica*) -- I prefer the white ones only, often called snow hawthorns. The pink ones tend to get too leggy for my purposes. The white ones (or snow hawthorns) stay in a compact, rounded growing form. They have a beautiful spring flower, but it is such a short bloom season that it's not a plant you purchase because of its flowering ability. These make a perfect low-profile hedge that will never get above 3 feet tall.

**Texas Sage** (*Leucophyllum frutescens*) – This is the one shrub, besides the elaeagnus, that has such distinctly silver leaves. If a Texas sage is taken care of properly, it can produce a striking rounded shrub with stunning orchid-lavender, bell-shaped flowers. This plant also tolerates poor soil. Because it is so drought and heat tolerant, the Texas sage is often the last plant standing in a landscape that has been completely ignored.

**Bulbine** (*Bulbine sp.*)– This is another "out-of-category" plant for this chapter. First, it's definitely not a shrub by definition and it's not even really a bulb. It's actually a true perennial for the Gulf Coast. Bulbine that works so well for Gulf Coast landscapes is affectionately referred to as Tangerine bulbine. It works so well, not just because of its unique growth pattern – a clumping pattern -- but because of the yellow-orange (thus, the tangerine description) combination in the blooms. It also has a somewhat succulent look when viewed close-up. It is a profuse bloomer too. I like it as the lowest stage of color-tiering, but bulbine can also do equally as well as a containerized shrub. In mild winters bulbine has been known to bloom all year. The bulbine works best in full sun, but can work in light shade as well.

**Brunfelsia** (*Brunfelsia australis*) – We commonly refer to the Brunfelsia as the Yesterday-Today-Tomorrow plant. That's because its beautifully fragrant blooms go from dark purple to lavender to white in a three day period. This almost has a tropical look to the leaves and the first purple flowers. The downside to this shrub is that it can get serious freeze damage unless protected on seriously cold nights. But it can bloom from April through October. It prefers a mostly filtered light to mostly shade environment, however, brunfelsia can tolerate a few hours of early morning sun. As such, brunfelsia makes a great shrub for a southern or southeast exposure that can be protected from north and northwest winds and freezing temperatures. It should reach only 5 feet in height at maturity.

**Esperanza/Yellow Bells** (*Tecoma stans*) – If you look at garden books for Texas and the Gulf Coast from just 10 years ago, you find almost no references to yellow bells/esperanza. But the popularity of this plant as an ornamental shrub has grown rapidly in just the past few years. While found in the wild of drought-ravaged areas, you still have to be protective of esperanza because it can suffer serious freeze damage. In more northern parts of each state that might be considered a part of the Gulf Coast, this plant has to be used more as an annual or container plant that can be moved into warmer winter quarters. The striking, tubular 2 1/2-inch bright yellow flowers are highlighted by the attractive, shiny, green foliage and continue through the heat of the summer. The flowers have an odd but pleasing fragrance and also provide nectar for bees. If you've ever been to South Texas in the hottest months of the year, this is the one plant that blooms profusely the hotter it gets. In Mexico, a beer was prepared from its roots; it has also been used for a variety of medicines in many Central American rural areas.

**Sweet Olive** (*Osmanthus fragrans*) – This is another one of those versatile plants for upright, semi-columnar growing conditions. Sweet olive can get as high as 14 feet at maturity but can be trained to be no wider than 4 to 6 feet as well. Most people use sweet olive as "entrance" plants by front doors and walkways mainly because of its fragrant blooms. Unfortunately, the blooms only last for a few months, usually from February through May. If you want to direct the growth in a more upright fashion, this plant should be tip pruned all year long.

**Natal Plum** (*Carissa macrocarpa*) – This is another one of those plants that work great for the Gulf Coast, but are rarely found in nurseries and garden centers. In fact, the closer you actually get to the "coast," the better this plant does. It produces a star jasmine-like bloom that is quite fragrant and has a rich green, leathery look to the leaves. It produces a fruit that is actually edible. Along the coast (within 50 miles of the actual shore), it is one of the faster growing shrubs. It tolerates poor soil, doesn't have many pest problems and is drought tolerant. So, why is it not more available? It's probably because it is such a "coastal" specimen, therefore, a majority of the mass merchandising nurseries in the bigger cities don't carry something so specific.

**Altheae/Althea/Rose of Sharon** (*Hibiscus syriacus*) – I like to refer to the Althea/Rose of Sharon as a cross between a hibiscus and crape myrtle. While it is technically in the Hibiscus family, it seems to suffer many of the same maladies and will lose its leaves in winter much like a crape myrtle. The Althea is the perfect flowering shrub for the lazy gardener in all of us because it takes full sun and doesn't require much care after it's established, unless it gets an insect infestation. A fully-grown Althea can reach 10 to 12 feet high at maturity and can produce a number blooms all summer long and well into the first frost. Varieties can be purple, lavender, white, pink, red and salmon-colored. There are single and double blooming varieties of Altheas, too. Like a crape myrtle, (because it is deciduous) it will lose its leaves in the winter. However, Altheas bounce back immediately after the early spring pruning they require.

LET'S JUMP OUT OF THE CONTEXT OF SHRUBS FOR THE NEXT FEW PLANTS

**Giant Liriope** (*Liriope Muscari*) -- Liriope actually falls into the groundcover category. Since most people know what monkey grass is, the best way to describe liriope to the new gardener is that is looks like monkey grass on super steroids. It will produce a bit of a purple bloom on a thin stalk several times throughout the year, and if kept well-watered and protected from afternoon sun, will stay evergreen year-round. The more it grows, however, the more it will need to be thinned out/separated from year to year. In shady to filtered light environments, liriope is a great addition to the color-tiering system. It also makes a great alternative to grass in areas that are getting too much shade and turfgrass simply won't grow anymore.

**Aztec Grass** (*Liriope muscari* 'Aztec') – While Aztec grass is a variegated version of giant liriope, it is truly its own cultivar. This is important to note because Aztec grass does so much better along the Gulf Coast rather than its first cousin of simple variegated liriope. If you like the idea of the color-tiering system, you will absolutely love Aztec grass, because of its cream and green striping. Imagine a triple tiered bed with something dark green in the back, something like a Lorapetalum in the middle with dark purple and green leaves, and then the Aztec grass in front. Talk about distinctive color separation.

**Asparagus Fern/Foxtail Ferns** (*Asparagus 'Sprengeri'*) – Like so many of the groundcovers that work along the Gulf Coast, if you can keep asparagus and foxtail ferns from being hammered by late afternoon sun, these kind of ferns will thrive in almost any light condition. However, they need excellent drainage and will turn sour if the roots stay wet for too long. Asparagus fern has prickly arching light green fronds with insignificant white flowers followed by red berries. Foxtail ferns have a more columnar-tubular look to their upright growth pattern. But, it is the unique lime-green coloring that makes these ferns stand out in a landscape. If they turn yellow, they are probably not getting enough sun or enough water. In many cases of nutrient deficiencies, they green up quickly with a jolt of organic fertilizers like fish emulsion.

**Variegated Privet/Vicaryi Privet** (*Ligustrum vicaryi*) – I have mixed emotions about this shrub. I've seen many well-established ones that I just love, yet the younger ones look so scraggly to me that I'm not sure I have the patience to have them in my landscape. However, because of their wonderful cream/gold/green/ variegation, they make a wonderful alternative to our landscape. In good soil, this is normally a fast growing shrub that will max out at 5 feet in height. But again, it's the striking foliage of cream/gold/green that makes it such a great "contrast" plant.

**Japanese Blueberry-**Shogun Series (*Elaeocarpus decipiens*) – This is one of those plants that didn't really exist in Gulf Coast garden centers until a few years ago. It's also mostly considered a small tree by other horticultural definitions. I like it as a big shrub alternative to the old standards of red tips and ligustrums. It's the ornamental effect of its older leaves turning bronze to bright red before they drop that most people will like. The Japanese blueberry acts mostly like an evergreen plant. Still, these shrubs can suffer light freeze damage if the temperatures stay below 20 degrees for long periods. Of all the plants listed, this one can get the tallest at over 20 feet at its maturity. However, if you trim it back two to three times a year, you can keep a Japanese blueberry at a specific height for screen purposes.

**Bottlebrush** (*Callistemon spp.*) – The Bottlebrush, in my opinion, is one of the most "under-utilized" shrubs in Gulf Coast landscapes. By its name alone, you probably know exactly what I'm talking about, in that the blooms look like maroon-colored bottle brushes. These bottlebrush blooms come in waves throughout the year. Plus, bottlebrush blooms will attract hummingbirds year-round. This is a drought tolerant plant with unique foliage and blooms that reach a mature height of 10 feet. However, it can take several years to get there.

**Yaupon** (*Ilex vomitoria*) -- I list this plant at the very end for two reasons. First, I think it is entirely over-used in Gulf Coast landscapes. On the other hand, it is still one of the hardiest shrubs we can ever use. Actually, it's the dwarf yaupons that are over-used in my opinion (*Ilex vomitoria 'nana'*). The standard yaupon is the one that can make an excellent small tree at the corner of a landscape. It is a true Texas native as well. Weeping yaupon is probably my favorite of all the varieties available. The dwarf version is probably second only to the Indian hawthorn as the most often-used low profile shrub. This is the one you see "rounded" in most professionally manicured landscapes. The larger version, which can reach 15 feet at maturity, can also be shaped at the top in a rounded form just as easily.

## YAH-YAH PLANTS

You may have noticed that some of the acid-loving stalwarts of Gulf Coast landscapes are not included in my Top 30 list. There are two reasons for this. 1.) They are not always the "easiest-to-care-for" plants out there, and require lots of molly-coddling in terms of feeding, insects and diseases. 2.) Their "limited" blooming time always makes me wonder whether they are worth the effort. But, I do put them in a secondary category all by themselves and affectionately refer to them as Yah-Yah plants.

Again, in deference to my many Greek friends, this is not a rip off of Yia Yia (meaning grandmother in Greek). I call them Yah-Yah plants, because they all fall into the acid-loving plant category and they all have some kind of phonetic YAH at the end of the name.

## Hydrangea, Camellia, Azalea, Gardenia

If you are interested in any of these harder-to-care-for plants, there are some basic elements worth remembering. First, it wouldn't hurt to plant them in a raised bed of azalea soil. Like the rose soils, so often referred to in this book, azalea soil is a blend of soil, sand and humus. It's just that the humus in the azalea soil is more geared for the acid-loving plants.

Next, since they are acid-loving plants by definition, they will all respond to the basic acid loving plant foods that almost always say azalea/camellia food. How often you feed them is dependant on the plant in question, so please read the label for instructions. Most of these specially designed foods are infused with something to acidify the soil as well as a jolt of iron for greening-up purposes. Acid-loving plants can't green up with iron alone unless the pH of the soil is at 6.6 or lower.

**Azaleas** (Azalea spp.) -- This is long-standing staple plant in many Gulf Coast landscapes, but not necessarily one of my favorite shrubs. Sure they have beautiful blooms in early spring, but that bloom season lasts for one month and that's if I'm being generous. The problem with most azaleas along the Gulf Coast is if they are planted in poor soils of the vast majority of new builder homes. New homeowners want the look they see in more established neighborhoods, but it is such a long struggle to get there, especially if starting with anything less than azalea soil. Plus, there is a technique in planting azaleas that means lightly tearing the roots apart so they will grow laterally in the soil, like they want to. All too often, people plant them in a hole the size of the root ball not understanding what kind of problems this causes for the plant's health. Another pratfall for new azaleas is when people plant them where they are getting full sun. Azaleas thrive better in filtered light or where they get only morning sun. There's also a new trend for a new variety of azaleas that bloom several times a year. I loved the idea at first, when they hit the market around 1997. Since then, they have been a total disappointment, in my opinion. While these supposed multi-bloomers do actually provide three distinct blooming seasons, their foliage production, or lack thereof, is what makes them so frustrating. They always look devoid of leaves, as if they are suffering from some disease.

**Gardenia** *(Gardenia jaminoides fortuniana)* – These are probably the most fragrant of all the shrubs (Top 30 & Yah-Yah) I can suggest. And much like the azaleas, gardenias are higher-than-normal on the maintenance scale. They require a bit more sun than the azalea, but can't handle the brutal late-afternoon sun either. They are frustrating when you can't get them to bloom (which happens quite often), despite following the instructions on azalea/camellia fertilizers. Gardenias also suffer easily from chlorosis (iron deficiencies).

**Hydrangea** *(Hydrangea macrophylla)* -- This is possibly the "showiest" of all the Yah- Yah plants. Hydrangeas crave northern exposures, but also need to be protected from the blazing heat of late afternoon sun. Most people prune them at the wrong time of the year and end up with no blooming action. Alhtough they look scraggly and leafless in the winter, they shouldn't be pruned until after the normal blooming season of April through June. If you want more blue flowers, you need to increase the acidity of the soil by sprinkling aluminum sulphate or sulphur. If you want more pink-colored hydrangea blooms, you should increate the alkalinity by adding dolomitic lime.

**Camellia** *(Camellia japonica)* -- Like azaleas and gardenias, a Camellia is better suited to having morning sun, but filtered light the rest of the day. Camellias are quite simply the best choice for a blooming plant in months we don't normally have much color in the landscape – January to March. In days of yesteryear, there used to be camellia societies and garden tours featuring the camellia in many Gulf Coast communities, speaking to its popularity. That popularity has waned over the last 50 years. While there are also *Camellia sasanqua* varieties available too, they are more susceptible to freeze damage, so keep an eye out for the better *Camellia japonica* varieties. Like the gardenia, it can get very frustrating when a Camellia produces what looks like a lot of blooms, but few of them open up. There is a GIB hormone treatment (gibberellin acid) when this phenonmon occurs, but there is no guarantee that it will produce blooms either.

## Honorable Mention Plants

If you see any of these at a nursery or garden center, and you like them, then by all means GIVE 'EM A TRY!

Abelia

Aspidistra (Cast Iron Plant)

Boxleaf Euonymus

Burford Holly

Crape Myrtles (shorter varieties)

Japanese Boxwood

Oregon Grape Holly

Spirea (Bridal Wreath)

Texas Mountain Laurel

Taxus

Viburnum

## PLANTS TO AVOID

I never was on a debate team in high school or college, but I feel confident that I can explain to anyone who will lend me an ear why you shouldn't plant any of these next plants into a Gulf Coast landscape.

You may disagree. That, to me, is an open invitation to a debate on the radio program some day.

**Red Tip Photinias** (*Photinia Fraseri glabra*) - Fungal leaf spot mercilessly ravages this plant as well as cotton root rot. If you don't mind getting out with a fungicide several times a year, then by all means you can plant red tips. But, I think there are better alternatives like the Japanese blueberry and the Texas wax myrtle, if you're looking for a potentially big hedge row. Yes, the reddish leaves in spring are beautiful, but the potential problems are worth looking elsewhere. Every couple of years some new grower claims they have a new hybrid that will not suffer from the fungal leaf spot. To date, none of the newer introductions have actually lived up to that promise. There is one small hope. Finally, there are growers in Texas that are actually propagating a variety here that I hope can adapt to our heat and humidity and not be susceptible to the disease. In the past, almost all varieties came from California growers, which may explain why they always succumb to the disease.

**Wax Leaf Ligustrum** (*Ligustrum japonicum*) – Much like the red tips, the ligustrums are ravaged with fungal leaf spot and root rot diseases. The alternatives are many, such as wax myrtles, Japanese blueberry, cleyera and elaeagnus. While ligustrum may not be as heavily ravaged by disease, it was overused for so many years in early suburban landscapes that it really doesn't speak to anything "innovative" for Gulf Coast landscapers these days. Maybe 20 years from now, I might see a trend back towards their use, if the fungal diseases are more easily managed.

**Golden Euonymus** – Yuck! Ick!! Pitooey!!! Those are the three nicest words I can use for the infamous golden euonymus. People are first attracted to this plant because of the distinctly yellow leaves mixed with green. But, this plant can't help but become overwhelmed with euonymus scale, an insect that can quietly suck the life from this plant. Sometimes it doesn't matter how much insecticide you use, the scale just keeps on proliferating on euonymus. Plus, it is a notoriously slow grower. Anytime I see a new builder home landscape with these, I think 1.) They were on sale at the wholesale nursery and cheap plants make for higher profit margins on wham-blam, slap-em-in landscapes 2.) That landscaper doesn't know anything about landscaping on the Gulf Coast.

**Pampas Grass** – This is a tough one to hate, because it grows so fast and looks so different. But, I hate them because I'm a golfer. All golfers know what I'm talking about when you lose a golf ball in the middle of pampas grass. OUCH! If, you need a good privacy hedge that is unique and will grow relatively fast, you have some tacit approval here. But just remember, that they almost always have to be trimmed way back each spring to remove winter damage and there's about three months out of the year that they look just awful. Plus, there are better ornamental grasses for landscapes, such as purple fountain grass, muhly and lemongrass.

**Barberry** – I realize that most people choose the Pigmy Barberry because of its maroon-crimson leaves. But that thing looks so dead for so many months out of the year, because of its deciduous nature. I simply can't have a dead looking shrub in my yard for 5-6 months out of the year, no matter how unusual the leaves are.

# Quick Reference Guides
# For Plants/Shrubs
## - *Mostly Sun*
## - *Filtered Light*
## - *Mostly Shade*

# QUICK REFERENCE GUIDES

**Best Plants for Mostly Sun**

Abelia

Aztec Grass

Boxleaf Euonymus

Bottlebrush

Burford Holly

Coppertone Loquat

Crape Myrtles

Duranta

Dwarf Wheeler Pittosporum

Elaeagnus

Esperanza/Yellow Bells

Hibiscus

Indian Hawthorn

Japanese Boxwood

Japanese Blueberry – Shogun Series

Junipers

Lily of the Nile

Lorapetalum

Muhly

Nandina

Natal Plum

Needlepoint Holly

Oleander

Purple Fountain Grass

Red Tip Photinia (careful)

Privet

Rose of Sharon (Altheae)

Sago Palm

Spirea

Sweet Olive

Texas Mountain Laurel

Texas Sage

Texas Wax Myrtle

Viburnum

Waxleaf Ligustrum (careful)

Yaupon Holly

## Best Plants for Filtered Light to Light Shade

(You may notice some similar plants from the Sun Loving List. That means they should work in either instance.)

Agapanthus/Lily of the Nile

Asparagus Fern/Foxtail Fern

Aztec Grass

Azaleas

Blue Plumbago

Boxleaf Euonymus

Brunfelsia (Yesterday-Today-Tomorrow)

Camellia

Cleyera

Dwarf Nandina/Compacta

Gardenia

Giant Liriope

Hydrangea

Japanese Yew

Lorapetalum

Needlepoint Holly

Pigmy Date Palm

Pyracantha

Sago Palm

Spirea

Sweet Olive

Viburnum

Texas Wax Myrtle

Yaupon Holly

## Plants for Mostly Shade

Besides the shrubs listed below, you can always grow a number of groundcovers that love shade. Examples: Asiatic jasmine, Algerian ivy, English ivy, pachysandra and monkey grass. These choices are especially important in areas where the shade is so dense and the roots from trees so competitive that the only option you might have is to use groundcovers.

Aspidistra (Cast Iron Plant)

Azaleas

Brunfelsia

Cleyera

Dwarf Nandina

Giant Liriope

Holly Fern

Japanese Yew

Needlepoint Holly

Oregon Grape Holly

Sago Palms

Texas Wax Myrtle (could get leggy)

Viburnum (Sandankwa only)

# Chapter Four-

## Turfgrass Care for the Gulf Coast

*a.k.a. The Grass is always greener on your side of the fence*

# TURFGRASS CARE

As we step into the new Millennium, it has been said that lawn care is the equivalent to the jousting and duels of yesteryear. You know, weed whackers at 20 paces. Speaking of yesteryear, it's also suggested that the modern day lawn is the equivalent of a great, green moat. Although you may think of it as open and inviting, our lawns essentially separate us from our neighbors. Gulf Coast front yards, in particular, are not a land of fences and hedges, unlike our European brethren, to delineate our front yards. And that is why it is so important to keep that turf grass green and manicured.

May I suggest that a rich, green lawn is a sign of marking our territory? Don't laugh! I'm not talking about dogs marking territory. I'm talking about modern-day territorialism. Like automobiles, homes and fine clothes, a well-manicured lawn also represents success for some folks. Is it a sign of power? Is it a sign of pride? Or, is it a sign of control? Personally, I think it is a sign that individually we know how to take care of our own business. Thus, our lawns allow us to flaunt our success – to fuss and preen and show off! Oddly enough, we do all this work knowing that the turf portions of our front landscapes are virtually identical.

It has been my job as the radio garden guru to help people succeed with their landscaping in general. However, more than 50 percent of the questions I answer always seem to center on lawn care. That's why I came up with a schedule for lawn care that I'm confident will work on just about any lawn, in any part of the Gulf Coast, but was originally tailored for Houston. Now, you too, will be well-armed in this modern day duel with the neighbors. Before I give you the basic components of a fertilization schedule that you can use with confidence, there are some tenets of lawn care that are worth discussing.

## FERTILIZATION

There are three schools of thought on fertilization of Gulf Coast area lawns no matter what turf grass you have. The three methods are Slow-Release, High Nitrogen-based, or Organic Compost-based.

My personal favorite is the Slow-Release fertilization program because it provides us with consistency and saves us a bunch of money. The beauty of the Slow-Release schedule is that you can jump in at any point. However, if you haven't applied any rules of this fertilization schedule for some time, or never, it will take a full year to generate the best results. But, I promise you will see great results if you follow the schedule for a year or more.

And the nice thing about this schedule is that it works on just about every type of turf we can use on the Gulf Coast. St. Augustine, Bermuda, Zoysia, Centipede, Paspallum, Carpetgrass and Buffalograss.

The Slow-Release schedule is based on using the 3-1-2/4-1-2 ratio fertilizers recommended by turf grass researchers at Texas A&M University. The ratio is defined by three elements: Nitrogen, Phosphorous and Potassium or N-P-K. Without getting involved in too much scientific data, suffice it to say, that the best fertilizers in our area have more nitrogen than phosphorous and potassium. We already have too much Phosphorous in our soils, which is why you rarely see research that recommends 13-13-13 fertilizers for turf, as was once the norm in the Houston area. A 15-5-10 ratio is a perfect definition of a 3-1-2. Others that fall into the slow-release category are 19-4-10, 19-5-9, 18-4-6, 21-5-10 and 21-7-14.

High Nitrogen-based fertilizers will require more irrigation than the 3-1-2 ratios mentioned above. Examples of High Nitrogen fertilizers are 33-2-5, 29-3-5 and 29-3-4. These are also known as "hot" fertilizers which is why they need ample amounts of water. This ensures the release of nitrogen (the first number in the ratios) and keeps you from "burning" the lawn.

The Organic-Compost applications are just that – using composted humus, organic fertilizers or composted manure as your fertilizer. The common problems in Organic Compost fertilizations are 1. They are hard to spread with broadcast spreaders. 2. They cover much less square footage. Thus, you have to buy 3 to 5 times as much to cover an area that one bag of synthetic slow-release fertilizer will cover. 3. They smell like composted manure. 4. They can take up to two years to achieve ultimate results. But if staying organic is your goal, there are plenty of organic fertilizers on the market. There are also a few formulated organic fertilizers that can, with difficulty, be used in broadcast spreaders.

## HERBICIDES

When I talk to people about the use of herbicides, I'm almost always talking about Pre-Emergent herbicides. These are herbicides that will keep weeds from ever being a problem. If Pre-Emergent herbicides are put down at the correct times of the year, rarely should you have to use Weed & Feed fertilizers or Post-Emergent herbicides. Pre-Emergent herbicides are a barrier to the germination of weed seeds.

Weed & Feed fertilizers, which have a herbicide built in, are very effective but at the same time dangerous to root systems of trees and shrubs. Plus, Weed & Feed herbicides move so easily through the soil and to the street that they also pose a contamination threat in groundwater runoff.

However, there are times that a poorly cared for lawn will need a Weed & Feed. If this is the case, I normally recommend a once-a-year application in March. Even if you feel that you have to use a weed & feed application, it is still highly recommended that you come back to the slow-release schedule on the next fertilization.

On the safer side of this issue, if weeds are already a problem, I strongly advocate the use of Post-Emergent herbicides. These are normally a liquid application and in most cases are Ready-To-Use (RTUs), in as much as you hook the RTU bottle on the end of a hose and apply directly to the offending weeds.

## FUNGICIDES

Since most of the lawns along the Gulf Coast are of the St. Augustine variety, we sadly must fight off a myriad of fungal diseases. Most of them are easy-to-treat with topical fungicides. The bane of most St. Augustine lawns is a disease commonly referred to as Brownpatch

(*Rhizoctonia solani*). Brownpatch is normally a problem in the months of August through November and is characterized by circular patterns of yellow to browning grass blades. Furthermore, Brownpatch is almost always associated with areas that have drainage problems.

Fortunately, it can be prevented from ever being a problem by following the schedules later in this chapter with the use of systemic or preventive fungicides. Other fungal ailments like Fairy Ring (usually indicated by half-moon shaped yellowing grass followed by mushrooms), can be treated with any number of topical fungicides. Gray Leaf Spot (Piricularia grisea) causes oval or circular, tan-colored lesions on leaf blades. This fungal disease is almost always associated with overly wet St. Augustine and can also be treated with a number of topical fungicides.

The easiest fungal disease to control is commonly known as Slime Mold. Interestingly, Slime Mold is probably the most unusual looking fungal disease causing small patches of grass to look as if it has been spray-painted with an oily-based, salt-and-pepper-coating on the leaf blades. Again, this is easy to brush away with a broom dipped into a water and fungicide mix. For years, I've recommended Consan-based fungicides for this wash mixture.

## PESTICIDES

Chinch Bugs!!! These are two of the scariest words for most Gulf Coast homeowners. We also have trouble with grub worms, cutworms and sod webworms. For the most part, chinch bugs are the most common critter we must control with pesticides. With the eventual phase-out of commonly used pesticides Dursban and Diazinon, you may be wondering what can be used in the future. Fear not! There are plenty of new alternatives and even some organic controls that will work just as effectively. Better yet, the best way to prevent chinch bugs, which I will discuss in detail later, is to keep a yard well watered.

Synthetic Pyrethroids to look for as replacements in the future are Deltamethrin, Cypermethrin, Resmethrin, Pyrmethrin, Fipronil and Imidacloprid. Organic controls that have shown promise are Orange Oil Extracts (D-Limonine) and Cedar Oils. Another key to keeping chinch bugs at bay is keeping a healthy, well-watered lawn by following the fertilization schedule. Chinch bugs will not feast on a lawn that is thick and healthy. They are opportunistic and feast only on stressed areas of St. Augustine turf.

It is my philosophy that you don't put out pesticides to "prevent" insect problems. Besides, a healthy yard is the best defense again most insect pressures.

# SLOW-RELEASE SCHEDULE (Randy's Choice)

The Slow-Release schedule is comprised of four fertilizer applications, three herbicide applications, two fungicide applications and one iron supplementation (optional).

**Early February Through Early March** - Pre-Emergent Herbicide -- This will help prevent weed seeds from germinating February through April.

**End of February-First of March** - Apply a fast-acting 15-5-10. (Example: Nitro Phos Imperial) This will give you a quick green up a month before the slow release part.

**April** - Slow release 3-1-2 ratios (Examples: Nitro Phos Super Turf 19-4-10; Easy Gro Premium 19-5-9; Fertilome Southwest Greenmaker 18-4-6; Southwest Fertilizer Premium Gold 15-5-10; Mr. C's Finest 21-5-10.) *These recommendations are for the Gulf Coast region that incorporates the Houston area. However, many varieties from Nitro Phos to Fertilome are available in many other counties and other states.*

**May - Pre-Emergent Herbicide**. This will help prevent weed seed from germinating May through August.

**July – Slow release 3-1-2 ratios** (Examples: same as in April)

**End of August** - Fungicide **Preventative**. Use systemic fungicides to prevent Brownpatch. Examples: Turfcide Terrachlor, Nitro Phos PCNP Terrachlor, Safe-T Green, Fertilome Liquid Systemic Fungicide, any Myclobutanil product like Fertilome F-Stop or Green Light Fung-Away, or any Systemic Bayleton.

**End of September** - **Fungicide Preventative**. Use systemic fungicides again.

**October – Winterizer Formulas** of the aforementioned products.

**End of October through November – Pre-Emergent Herbicide**. This will help prevent weed seed from germinating December and January.

## ORGANIC –COMPOST SCHEDULE

Consists of four organic-compost fertilizations, two natural herbicide applications and one natural fungicide application.

As I mentioned earlier, organic fertilizations can end up being a little more tedious and costly, simply because most organic fertilizers only cover an average of 1,500 to 2,500 square feet per bag. Most synthetic fertilizers can cover 5,000 to 7,500 square feet.

**February/March** - Organic compost or formulated organic fertilizers. Examples: Lady Bug Natural, Bradfield's, Maestro Gro's Texas Tee, Gardenville's Soil Food, Medina Granular Organic, Back to Nature Compost or Back to Nature Composted Poultry Litter.

**February** – Corn Gluten Meal as Herbicide. This is a natural way of preventing weeds, but is hard to find.

**May/June** - Organic compost or formulated organic fertilizers.

**August/September** - Organic compost or formulated organic fertilizers.
**August/September** – Agricultural Corn Meal as Fungicide. (Different from the store bought kind and different from the corn gluten meal used as pre-emergent herbicide) Even harder to find than Corn Gluten Meal.

**October/November** - Organic compost or formulated organic fertilizer as a winterizer.

**November** - Corn Gluten Meal as Herbicide. This is a natural way of preventing weeds, but is hard to find.

# WEED CONTROL & PREVENTION

If you've looked closely at the previous schedules, you know I'm a huge proponent of PRE-EMERGENT herbicides. While the best way to prevent weeds, in general, is to have a thick, healthy and well-watered lawn, you can severely prevent weed seeds from germinating by following the PRE-EMERGENT part of the fertilization schedule. However, many people forget that part of the schedule more than I like to admit.

Plus, Mother Nature can deal us an ugly blow from time to time. Homeowners who put down the PRE-EMERGENT HERBICIDES can have them washed away with continual rains. After such rains, the homeowner fails to lay down the pre-emergent herbicide again. Remember, however, one of my gardening maxims: "It's never too late to do the right thing". This is very important when applying PRE-EMERGENT herbicides. In fact, with the advancements in technology of these pre-emergent herbicides, it has become so much easier.

Years ago, when the first commercially available pre-emergent herbicide hit the retail market, you had to put one down to block grassy weeds, like Betasan. Then, you had to put down a pre-emergent specific to broadleaf weeds, like Portrait or Gallery. Today, there are a number of 2-in-1 pre-emergent herbicides on the market, like those containing Barricade or Dimension.

So, what if you forgot the pre-emergent application, or what if Mother Nature was cruel and washed them away? Well, then you will have weeds, especially during the months of February through April. This is when we use a myriad of POST-EMERGENT HERBICIDES. Interesting to note: Most of the broadleaf weeds that trouble us in early spring will wither away the hotter it gets. The same can be said for poa anna, the one true grassy weed that hits in January through March.

The best POST-EMERGENT herbicides for the Gulf Coast contain a combination of Trimec and 2-4D. The better and more well-known varieties are Fertilome Weed Out, Green Light Wipeout and Bonide

Weed Beater for Southern Lawns. It's also worth noting that many of the more national brands of broadleaf weed killers are very detrimental to St. Augustine lawns. So, it's important to read the labels and make sure they are safe for use. Broadleaf weed killers used on bermudas, bluegrasses and fescues will kill St. Augustine, so be very careful.

Once grassy weeds are up (with the exception of poa anna), they are nearly impossible to control, without killing surrounding grasses. That's why it's imperative to control grassy weeds with PRE-EMERGENT controls. POST-EMERGENT control on grassy weeds is relegated to the non-selective herbicides that kill all grasses like Eraser, Finale, Killzall and Roundup. Let's use the much-dreaded Crabgrass as an example. If you have Crabgrass, you can either dig them up or treat them with a non-selective herbicide. If you do the latter, then you need to dig out the dead area and bring in some new dirt or new pieces of sod. After all that, it is also essential to put down the PRE-EMERGENT herbicide on the new area, and block any possible seeds from germinating.

Sedges are a whole different game. You may know them better as Nutgrass. Did I hear a collective YIKES? Nutgrass can be controlled by some 2-in-1 PRE-EMERGENT HERBICIDES, but it's certainly not a 100 percent control, considering that they are sedges. There are two very good herbicides on the market for control of nutgrass/nutsedge. One is called Image and should only be used on turf grass during the months of April through June. Image can wipe out a St. Augustine yard if used at the wrong times of the year. The other herbicide, though more expensive, is SedgeHammer. However, SedgeHammer can be used at almost any time of the year. (SedgeHammer used to be Manage.)

In recent years, another weed that has developed quite a notorious reputation along the Gulf Coast is Virginia Buttonweed. Image herbicide will help eliminate Virginia Buttonweed if applied at the right time of the year. Another new herbicide that has made inroads against Virginia Buttonweed is Fertilome's Weed Free Zone. However, this herbicide has some very important temperature restrictions. In fact, Weed Free Zone is best used during the winter months when the temperatures are not below 40 degrees and not above 75 degrees.

## MULCH MOWING VS. BAGGING

As disappointing as this may sound, if you fertilizer properly with this schedule, you're going to need to mow the yard more often than you ever have. Even so, why should you have to stop to unload grass into trash bags? Doesn't that seem like more work than you intended? That's why I love mulch-mowing. Yes, you can bag your grass clippings early in the spring and when there are leaves on the ground in fall. Mulch-mowing, by today's standards, is extremely beneficial to the yard because the pulverized grass disappears into the root zone and becomes something of a nitrogen-rich fertilizer.

Why people still bag grass clippings (only to put them at the curb for trash pick up) is beyond me. If you have a compost pile, you can bag your grass clippings for that particular use. But think about this: We already have over-stressed landfills, and oddly enough, some 25-30 percent of the trash going to the landfills in the spring and summer is YARD WASTE! At this point, while grass can break down in the landfill, plastic bags do not. Mulch-mowed grass, in my opinion, is not just good for the lawn it is the environmentally responsible thing to do.

**AERATE/AERATION** - Technically speaking, aeration is the naturally occurring process of air exchange between the soil and its surrounding atmosphere. Practically speaking, aeration is the process of mechanically removing small plugs of thatch and soil from the lawn to improve soil aeration. Textbooks often refer to the practices of soil aeration as soil cultivation (coring, spiking, and slicing). The aeration process is also commonly called core aeration in the lawn service industry and homeowners often refer to it as aeration. I'm a firm believer that most lawns should be aerated every few years; especially those with compacted soils. Even then, compacted soils could benefit from an aeration three years in a row. These days, you can rent core aerators at most big box stores. Or, hire a landscape company to do the work. You can even do it yourself through microbial sprays. Companies that you hire, normally use a core aeration machine that pulls plugs out of the ground. In my view, this is the best kind of aeration. There are some aerators that you can rent that simply push holes into the ground. The do-it-yourself microbial treatments use liquid or granular treatments that organically treat the soil. This is a gradual process and needs to be done consistently for several months. Here are list of benefits you get from a core aeration:

* Improves air exchange between the soil and atmosphere.

* Improves the soil water uptake.

* Improves the fertilizer uptake and use.

* Reduces water runoff and improves drainage.

* Improves turfgrass rooting.

* Reduces soil compaction.

* Enhances thatch breakdown.


## THATCH


Some of you may be asking: If I mulch-mow all the time, won't I get a thatch build up?

Thatch build up has grown to mythical proportions along the Gulf Coast. Again, if your mulch mower is pulverizing the grass to such an extent that it is disappearing into the root zone, you shouldn't have a problem with thatch. Even then, a once-a-year aeration also helps prevent a thatch build up. Many people think they have thatch when they see matted grass from freeze or residual Brownpatch damage. But that's not true thatch.


Thatch occurs when organic material is produced faster than it can decompose. Believe it or not, a certain amount of thatch is a good thing. That's because it works as a cushion for high-traffic areas and can be a good insulator from extreme temperatures. It also reduces water evaporation, which can be beneficial during the hot summer months.

The key is finding out if you have too much thatch. To do so, dig out a small square with dirt, roots and all. Look at the layer of organic material between the grass blades and the soil line. If it's thicker than ½ inch of organic matter, then aerate in the spring.

## SCALPING

Scalping is one of those issues that has evolved over the years thanks largely to advancements in mowers and fertilizer technology. I grew up in Houston, where my family (my uncle still does so to this day) "scalps" the lawn by lowering the lawn mower a good inch lower than the regular mowing height. The idea is to bag up all the dead grass blades from winter damage. Moreover, it helps open up the root systems to oxygen and sunshine. However, if you scalp too soon and a freeze comes, the root system is extremely vulnerable. That's usually why we scalp only when we are certain that there are no more freezes. Along the Gulf Coast, that is usually around mid-March.

With advancements in mower and fertilizers, however, scalping just isn't needed as it once was. The newer mowers mulch-mow the grass so well that there is little chance of thatch build up. Therefore, there is little need for the "vacuuming" up of debris. Fertilizer technology gives us the controlled-release style fertilizers and winterizers that keep many lawns greener longer.

### Randy's Lawn Care Tenets:

**Don't Buy Cheap Fertilizers:** Don't just look for the "cheapest" fertilizer. Just because a big box store has a tremendous price on fertilizer does not mean it's best for your yard. It could be chocked with fillers. It is far wiser to spend a couple of more bucks per bag for something designed for this region. Read the back of the bag: Where was it made?

**Mow St. Augustine Grass Tall:** Mow as tall as your lawn mower will allow, specifically for St. Augustine lawns. The taller the grass blade the better the moisture retention, the deeper the root establishment the less likely you'll get weeds, and the more likely you'll shade out bermuda grass. This is something that most people resist mainly because the uneducated homeowner mows much lower, and there is a certain peer pressure to keep the lawns at the same height. I say "make your neighbor come up to your level". Even if they won't or don't, at least you'll have the healthiest lawn

**Don't Use Weed & Feeds**: If you keep your yard healthy, mow tall and keep it well-watered, you will never need a weed & feed. That's because a healthy turf is the ultimate defense against weeds. Plus, don't forget the environmental threats of weed & feeds on tree roots and groundwater supplies. Lastly, there is a move afoot to take the Atrizine (the main ingredient in Weed & Feeds) chemical off the market. I say you should get use to not having it in the first place.

**Give the Schedule One Full Year**: If you have poor soil, this is a very important concept. I've encountered many people that give up on the schedule because they didn't get some kind of immediate gratification from it; the way high nitrogen fertilizers sort of do. You create more problems for the future with high nitrogen fertilizers, especially like the ones that are wrapped into weed & feeds. For best results, you have to give the schedule a full year. If you have decent soil you will see results much quicker. Remember, the organic schedule can often take two years to see ultimate results.

**The Importance of the Winterizer Fertilization**: If you talk to any turf grass expert, they will tell you philosophically that if you could choose only one time of the year to fertilize, the winterizer is the best and most important one. Please understand, I'm not telling you that this should be the only fertilization each year. I hope I'm convincing you how important the winterizer formula can be. While I'm a firm believer in the tenet "It's never too late to do the right thing", it can be too late to put down a winterizer once we've had our first freeze/frost.

**Watering/Irrigation Practices**: Basically, most lawns do well with what amounts to 1-inch of rain per week. That's assuming that temperatures are moderated as well. So, when the summer temperatures begin to rise, your irrigation times should be bumped up as well. Plus, there are many other factors that come into play as well like what kind of grass you have and the kind of irrigation system or sprinkler you use. However, these are the basics I've taught the general public for more than 10 years, which takes into consideration temperatures and rainfall:

* As noted, normal turf and landscapes in this area do fine with 1-1½ inches per seven-day week when daytime temperatures are in the 70s and 80s. So, if you are getting a consistent rain once a week, you should be fine.

* As daytime highs hit 88-92, you can probably up that to 1-1½ inches every four to five days.

* When temperatures exceed 93 degrees consistently (normally July-August), you should probably water every two to three days.

* The kind of grass you have is also very important. St. Augustine needs the most water, bermuda the next most, and zoysia far less than the previous two.

* Your soil, however, is ultimately the most critical factor. Clay or sandy soils not very well enriched with organic matter definitely need more water because they dry out quicker.

* Water early in the morning. That's when water pressure is best, there's less wind to evaporate the moisture, and the turf will have a store of water for the warm day ahead. If you have an automatic sprinkler, schedule it to run between 3 and 8 a.m.

* If you don't have an automatic system, start the sprinkler when you first get up. If you water at night, you run a higher risk of fungal diseases like brownpatch.

* How do you determine how much time it takes for your system to put out an inch of water? Place an empty tuna or cat food can at the farthest point the spray pattern reaches. When it fills up, that's how long it takes. Depending on the system, the time can range from 15-45 minutes.

* If it seems some of your neighbors don't run their sprinklers as much as you, it could be they have more organic matter in their soil.

* Finally, if you aren't mowing as tall as your lawnmower will allow, make the change today. Tall grass in good soil develops deeper roots which draws a larger volume of deep moisture, requiring less supplemental irrigation. Plus, lawns mowed tall provide shade for the soil surface.

* There is one caveat to all of the above. Newly sodded lawns need to be watered on a daily basis during the heat of the summer. The idea is to keep the "mud" wet under the root zone so it will break down

and allow the roots to establish in the soil below. Don't drown the new sod ... just keep it moist enough to soften the soil and help the roots grow down.

**Iron Supplements**:  Many people obsess over having a dark green lawn. The quickest, safest way to get that is with Iron Supplements. Interestingly enough, if your soil is highly alkaline, all the iron in the world won't do a thing if you don't have a slightly acid soil.  Mother Nature's rain gives us the slight acidity we normally need. On the other hand, if we are in a drought, you will need to use the iron supplements that boost the acidity of the soil, such as a complete Iron & Soil Acidifier.

**Getting Rid of Bermuda in St. Augustine**:  Most people with St. Augustine have bits and pieces of Bermuda in their lawn.  But when it's overwhelming, and all you want is St. Augustine, what do you do?  The obvious answer is to kill, till and replace it with new sod.  But, that's for extreme cases only.  Mowing as tall as your lawn mower will allow is usually the best answer.  Bermuda doesn't grow in shade and the taller the St. Augustine, the more it will shade out the lower-growing Bermuda. Keep your St. Augustine yard from suffering drought and/or chinch bug damage because those weakened areas are a perfect invitation to the opportunistic Bermuda seed.

**Adding a Surfactant**:  First, here's a definition of what a surfactant is/does:  A soluble compound that reduces the surface tension of liquids, or reduces interfacial tension between two liquids or a liquid and a solid. I emphasize the use of surfactants when trying to kill weeds.

Whether it's weeds, unwanted grass or brush, a surfactant is almost always essential in the herbicide mix because most of the water along the Gulf Coast is considered "hard".  As such, hard water tends to bead up and roll right off the leaf surface.  When you add a surfactant, you'll notice that there's a sheen on the leaf surface.  Thus, the herbicide is actually sticking to the leaf and doing its intended duty. There are two ways of adding a surfactant to most of the herbicides we use. The simple way is to add a bit of dish soap to the mix. The normal dosage is about a tablespoon per gallon of spray. Then, there are the professional grade surfactants like Hi Yield's Spreader Sticker.  They won't cause any suds, but they will break down the surface tension.  Even if the herbicide in question says it contains a surfactant, hedge your bet and add a bit more either with dish soap or the professional type.

**Types of Grasses and the Schedule**: I mentioned earlier that these fertilization schedules work on St. Augustine, Bermuda, Zoysia, Centipede, Carpetgrass, Paspalum and Buffalograss. You can follow the basics for each grass and you will succeed. However, here are the adjustments you need to keep in mind:

**Bermuda** – You should add an additional slow-release 3-1-2 /4-1-2 fertilizer into the mix. So, April, June and August will work as well as the 15-5-10 and the Winterizer.

**Zoysia** -- Once established, zoysia will require less fertilizer, less water, and probably no need for fungal control. But for its first year or two follow the basics of the schedule. Then, you can start eliminating some of the "applications", as set forth in the previously mentioned schedules. First, I would eliminate the fungal disease controls. Eventually, you can eliminate one of the fertilizations from a zoysia fertilization schedule.

**Carpetgrass** - Not the best variety for the Gulf Coast, but it will respond to the basics of the fertilizer schedule. Carpetgrass must have a highly acidic soil to maintain good health.

**Paspallum** – This is a relatively new version of grass that looks like a combination of Bermuda and Emerald Zoysia. This is perfect for true coastal landscapes that have a high salt content in the soil. Since it behaves a lot like Bermuda, you will probably need to add an additional fertilization to the mix as discussed with regards to Bermuda.

**Buffalograss** - I liken this to weakened and depressed Bermuda. I've never personally liked it, but along the coastal areas it is a good alternative. Like Zoysia, once established Buffalograss requires less water, fertilizer and probably zero fungal disease controls. The ultimate benefit of Buffalograss is that it only has to be mowed once every few weeks. Nevertheless, follow the basics of the schedule for the first year. Fungal controls are totally optional on this grass as is the iron supplement.

**\*\*\*\*\*\*\*\*\*\*\*\*\*\*\*\*\*\*\*\*\*\*\*\*\*\*\*\*\*\*\*\*\*\*\*\*\*\*\*\*\*\*\*\*\*\*\*\*\*\*\*\***

# Quick Reference Guide:

Basic Fertilization Schedule

February 1st -- Pre-Emergent Herbicides

March 1st  --  15-5-10 Quick Green Up

April 1st   -- Slow Release 3-1-2 / 4-1-2 Ratio Fertilizer

May 1st    -- Pre Emergent Herbicides

July 1st   -- Slow Release 3-1-2 / 4-1-2 Ratio Fertilizer

August    -- Brownpatch Control

August    -- Possible Iron Supplementation (Totally Optional)

September -- Brownpatch Control

Oct/Nov.   -- Pre-Emergent Herbicides

Oct/Nov.   -- Winterizer Fertilizer

**\*\*\*\*\*\*\*\*\*\*\*\*\*\*\*\*\*\*\*\*\*\*\*\*\*\*\*\*\*\*\*\*\*\*\*\*\*\*\*\*\*\*\*\*\*\*\*\*\*\*\*\***

# Chapter Five-

# Using Annuals in the Gulf Coast Landscape

# USING ANNUALS

For most gardeners, annuals mean flowers. Or put another way, they are the ones that we plug into a swath of the landscape one or two times a year. But a varied use of annuals is not only aesthetically pleasing, it's one of the easiest things we can do to the garden, because they grow so profusely and are relatively easy to care for. And while annuals like to spend their time producing seed, in hopes that they will come back season after season, that doesn't always happen in the Gulf Coast climate. Which is why using "annuals" is such an interesting proposition in landscapes along the Gulf Coast. While we want that splash of color year round, we really have to work at it a couple of times a year and simply re-invest. Personally, I think it's worth it. However, I'm here to tell you that you can spend far less than one hundred dollars each year if you'll follow the advice in this chapter. Of course, this is assuming that you live in a typically-sized home and don't have several thousands of square feet of landscaping in which to provide for.

The transient nature I speak of with the waning of annuals, during three distinctive growing seasons along the Gulf Coast, makes them the most flexible plant material we can work with. Why should we plant annual "X" every February, annual "Y" every June and annual "Z" each November? Yes, those are the three best times to cycle out such annuals, but do they always have to be in that order X-Y-Z?

The hardest thing to remember about annuals is how color relationships work. Just because you like this color and that color, doesn't mean they're going to necessarily work in your garden. That's because some colors clash and some colors complement each other. If you were to pick out an orange Gerber daisy, it falls on the color wheel as a warm color -- which is a feeling; not a physiological property. A blue/violet flower thus falls on the cool feeling of a color wheel. The reason this is important is because annual colors need to be juxtaposed to the warm or cool color of your house, deck or window sill. Another way to explain this, (remembering that we're **not** talking about physiological heat and cool) is if you have a warm colored brick house, a bunch of warm colors like red. yellow and orange make the area even warmer. If you planted violets, blues, yellows or pastels against that warm brick or wood, you've now got a considerably cooler (feeling) that will be much more inviting.

Another important consideration is that to the eye, cool colors tend to recede, and warm colors tend to advance. Or put another way, warm colors standout and shout, helping to bring a distant part of the yard into shaper focus. So, generally speaking, cool colors are good for close-up viewing and warm colors are good for dramatic further away displays.

No matter what colors you choose, mixing whites of whatever species is always a good contrast maker.

Cool colors:

> Yellow-Green
>
> Green
>
> Blue-Green
>
> Blue
>
> Blue Violet/Dark Purple
>
> Violet
>
> Light yellow
>
> Pink
>
> Anything Pastel

Warm Colors

> Darker Yellow
>
> Yellow-Orange
>
> Orange
>
> Red
>
> Red-Orange
>
> Red Violet
>
> Fuchsia Pink

## ANNUALS IN CONTAINERS

Even if you have lots of trees and a lack of beds under those trees, you can still produce annual displays by using containers. In fact, I think annuals and containers were actually made for each other. I personally have all my color in the backyard landscaping in containers.

Spring pots of primroses and pansies can give way to summer flowering marigolds and impatiens, and the golden mums in the fall can be replaced in mild winter climes with crops of hard annuals like nasturtium and pansies. Another good tip for working with containerized annuals is to purchase slightly used and differing sized pots. And I'm not just talking about terra-cotta clay pots. Use wooden crates, half whiskey barrels, concrete pots and pots with design. One of the newest crazes in gardening are glazed pottery.

Finally, once you get good with annuals and you want more and more to line your landscape, you'll learn which ones work best by seeds and at which times of the year to sow those seeds.

At the end of this chapter there is a list of annuals for the three seasons based on whether they do well in sun or shade environments. Mix these annuals, on a yearly basis, and you won't just have to plant petunias in spring, periwinkles in summer and pansies in the fall.

## COLOR POCKETS

The safest way I can recommend working with annuals is to use color pockets in a landscape and containerized annual plantings. I'm a big fan of color pockets, because it helps draw particular attention to certain parts of the landscape, but it helps save you loads of money, because you need far fewer flats. Plus, color pockets can be a focal point of your landscape in another way by using the "three-times-a-year" technique, mentioned earlier, to change out color schemes.

What most new gardeners (those owning their first home) try to do is make lines of annuals in their flower beds. This is usually a waste of money because in most cases the soil is not conducive to flowers, much less landscape shrubs. But it also doesn't give the "splash" or "striking" look most people are after.

If you take a flat of flowers and actually plant them in a concentrated area, you will get a much more noticeable color blast. When planting annuals in a so-called "color pocket" you can start them off only three inches apart and they will tend to grow together quickly and give that "mass" appeal of flowers.

If you take a flat of annuals and make a straight line at the front of a landscape bed, assuming you have good soil, it will take months to get the kind of impact in color that you get instantaneously with "color pockets."

Color pockets should be located by front entrances, sidewalks or at the corners of beds. Remember the discussion from the chapter about shrubs about "color-tiering" or landscape plants? Imagine two color pockets on each side of a properly color-tiered landscape. You have plenty of color with the three variations of the shrubs, and two concentrated areas of flowers on each side filled with the color. And you probably wouldn't need more than 2 flats, or 1 flat per pocket.

## FEEDING ANNUALS

20 years ago, it was all about the water-soluble plant foods like Miracle Gro. But thanks to innovations in the fertilizer industry we have a myriad of slow-release blooming plant foods that make growing annuals so easy. My favorite, for years, has been Nelson's Color Star from Nelson Plant Food.

e the first to introduce the "slow-release-blooming-plant-food" ilf Coast horticultural market. Dean Nelson has worked in his family's agricultural fertilizer business for years, but was asked by a landscaping buddy to develop a specific fertilizer for flower beds. This landscaper didn't want to have to feed these pockets of flowers every couple of weeks with a water-soluble plant food.

That's essentially how the slow-release type of blooming plant food came to the market. Now, it is possible to feed a pocket of annuals one time. You see, if you change out the color 3 times a year, you essentially have to feed them only when you plant them thanks to the controlled release ability of these plant foods.

There are others out there, but in my opinion nothing compares to Nelson's Color Star. However, if you can't find Nelson's Color Star, then just keep an eye out for anything that says "Controlled Release" for blooming plants. These slow-release styles are almost always in the granular form. And they should say "use every 3-4 months." Now, if you are the kind of gardener that doesn't mind getting out there and feeding the color pockets every two weeks, then there are plenty of water-soluble plant foods still available including Miracle Gro.

## *Total Sun Loving Annuals for Early Spring*

Alyssum   - Pink/Purple/White

English daisy - Pink/Purple/White

Geranium - Red/Pink/Purple/White

Larkspur - Orange/Yellow/Violet/Blue/White

Nasturtium - Red/Pink/Orange/Yellow/White

Petunias - Red/Pink/Orange/Yellow/Purple/White/Multi-Colored

Phlox - Red/Pink/Purple/White

Primrose - Red/Pink/Yellow/Blue/White

Snapdragons – Red/White/Orange/Yellow/Pink/Purple

Stock - Red/Pink/Purple/White

Sweet William - Red/Pink/White/Multi-Colored

Verbenas - Red/Pink/Purple/White/Multis

Zinnias - Red/Pink/Orange/Yellow/White/Multi-Colored

## *Total Sun Loving Annuals For Summer*

Amaranthus - Red/Copper/Green

Bachelor Buttons - Red/Pink/Orange/Purple/Blue/White

Dahlia - Red/Pink/Yellow/Purple/White/Multis

Foxglove - Red/Pink/Yellow/White

Hollyhocks - Red/Pink/Orange/Yellow/Purple

Marigolds - Orange/Yellow/White/Multis

Mexican Heather - Pink/Purple/White

Moss Rose (Portulaca) –
Red/Pink/Orange/Yellow/Purple/White/Multis

Periwinkle (Vincas) - Red/Pink/Purple/White/Multis

Purslane - Red/Pink/Orange/Yellow/Purple/White/Multis

(Tropicals)

Alamanda - Yellow

Bougainvillea - Red/Pink/Orange/Yellow/Purple/White/Multis

Copper Plant - Yellow/Orange/Copper (Blend)

## *Mostly Sun Loving Annuals for Fall*

Calendulas - Orange/Yellow/White

Dianthus - Red/Pink/Purple/White/ Multis

Dusty Miller - Green/Gray/White (Blend)

Johnny Jump-Ups - Yellow/Blue/Purple

Ornamental Kale Purple/Green/Gray (Blend)

Ornamental Cabbage -Red/Purple/Green (Blend)

Pansy - (Every Color Imaginable)

Snapdragons - Red/Pink/Orange/Yellow/Purple/White/Multis

Violas -Red/Yellow/Blue/Purple/White

## *Mostly Shade Loving Annuals for Spring And Summer*

Caladium - (Multi Colored Reds/Purples/Greens/Whites)

Coleus - (Multi Colored Reds/Purples/Pinks/Greens)

Impatiens - Red/Pink/Orange/Purple/White (Some Multis)

New Guinea Impatiens - Red/Pink/Orange/Purple/White (Some Multis)

Wax Begonias - Orange/Pink/Red/White

(Tropicals)

Croton (Color combos of Yellow, Orange, Red, Pink and Green)

## *Mostly Shade Loving Annuals for Fall/Winter*

Coleus (until the first freeze) coppers, bronzes, yellows, greens

Cyclamen – Pink/Red/White/Purple

Dianthus – Pink/Red/White

Impatiens (until the first freeze) – Red/Pink/Orange/White/Purple

New Guinea Impatiens (until the first freeze) – Red/Pink/Orange/Purple

Wax Begonias (Green leaf versions only) – Red/Pink/White

# Chapter Six-

# Much Ado about Mulch

## *"You can never have enough mulch!"* -- Randy Lemmon

That has been a personal and fundamental gardening principle for me and one many of my radio listeners have heard for over 10 years. When I wrote that maxim, it actually got me into a bit of trouble a few times. I'll explain about that trouble in just a moment. But I'll stick by it and wholeheartedly believe you can benefit from it, too. It's also one of those things that friends of mine in the business of horticulture and the business of broadcasting remember to this day.

A great example of that was when I appeared on the Debra Duncan show on Channel 13 in Houston. Debra helped break the ice with me in the make-up room by reciting my oft-repeated phrase, "You can never have enough mulch!" She sort of pointed her finger at me, with a slight wink, acknowledging that she listened to my recent advice on the radio.

Still, the main point about mulch is to use them whenever and wherever. Why? Here's my Top Ten List of beneficial things.

1. They are the First Line of Defense Against Weeds
2. They Help Conserve Moisture in the Spring
3. They Prevent the Soil Surface from Caking/Compacting
4. They Conserve Moisture in the Summer
5. They Help Insulate Roots During Drought Stress
6. They Help Insulate Roots During Freezes
7. They Conserve Moisture in the Winter
8. They Break Down into Useable Organic Matter
9. They Enhance the Aesthetics of the Garden
10. They Help Conserve Moisture in the Fall

To this day it boggles my mind that there are some people who re-mulch once a year, if they do it at all. I think there are three perfect times in a

calendar year in which to mulch the beds and trees etc.:  EARLY
SPRING, THE DEAD OF SUMMER and RIGHT BEFORE THE
HEART OF WINTER.

Let me break this down into more detail.  Let's start at the beginning of
the year and let's make the assumption that all nasty winter weather (or
what we think of as winter along the Gulf Coast) has run its course.   By
the end of February or the beginning of March, if you're not thinking
about the upcoming landscape work then your spouse probably is.  So,
when you go out to buy new plant material, this is the best time to stock
up on the your first round of mulch.

Here's where the first instance of,  "You can never have enough mulch!"
will come into play.  That's because few people ever get enough mulch.
So, on a typical landscape, I always recommend you buy at least four or
five more bags than you originally intended.  Few, if any average
gardener (or below average especially – tee-hee), ever picks up enough
bags of mulch.  That eventually means they will spread what they have
entirely too thin to make it last.  That is when a serious storm comes
through and washes the thin layer away.

The second time of the year that I contend a serious re-mulching should
take place is during the dead of summer.  By now, especially along the
Gulf Coast, daytime temperatures are consistently at 90 degrees or above
and drought stress is a real possibility.   Again, buy four or five more bags
than you think you need, unless you took the early spring advice and
already have a good idea of what it will take.  However, in many cases if
the beds are healthy and there hasn't been much run-off from rains, this
second mulching is usually just a top dressing.  Besides, it still may be a
good idea to have a few extra bags of mulch hanging around for "fill-in"
purposes.  Heavy rains, heavy foot traffic or heavy-handedness in the
garden could create a need for that "fill-in" bag or two. Which, of course,
falls right into that maxim of "You can never have enough mulch".

Finally, before winter sets in, mulch every part of the garden again.  This
nice new layer of mulch will really help the plants/shrubs/tree root
systems stay insulated from any serious freezing weather.  Plus, the water
retention/conservation may be even more important at this time of the

year. That's usually because many people flat out forget to keep irrigation practices going during the dead of winter – but that's a lecture for a different day, different chapter or different book. Again, this may just be the need for another top dressing to add to that which is already there.

# WHAT KIND OF MULCH SHOULD I USE?

I realize that this is actually the most often asked question I get regarding mulch. But, applying the mulch more often is actually the more important gardening principle for garden advice gurus like me. What "kind" of mulch is best for your garden or landscape is dependant on many things. While I do have my personal favorites, there are so many varieties and so many tastes that I think it's a personal decision to make. Nevertheless, I think we can cover just about anyone's likes and dislikes with these suggestions. Once again, we come to a Top Ten List.

**Shredded Hardwood Mulch** – There are actually two distinct hardwood mulches on the market. One is shredded fine enough that it is ready to be a compost amendment as well. The other hardwood mulch is more like chunks and pieces of hardwood with very little "shredding". That is why it is imperative to find the hardwood mulches that say SHREDDED on the label. The benefits of this mulch are many: It stays in place better than most, keeps a rich color longer than others, breaks down quicker into more of a compost and it could be the most cost-effective mulch by pricing standards. Some shredded hardwood mulches are known to get an ooze-like foam on the top layer of the mulch. This is simply a saprophytic fungus (a beneficial fungus by definition) and completely harmless to the mulch or neighboring plants. I'll explain more about this fungus later in this chapter.

**Shredded Pine Bark Mulch** – Much like the aforementioned Shredded Hardwood Mulch, Shredded Pine Bark Mulch can often come in two forms. Obviously, the SHREDDED variety works best for Gulf Coast gardening situations. Pine Bark Nuggets do not fall into this category. While still an attractive, dark style mulch, it does tend to float away easier than shredded hardwood mulches. Its ultimate benefit is for those people with lots of Yah-Yah plants. Pine bark mulches have a little more acid in them, as they break down in the soil.

**Mixed Mulch** (A Blend of Shredded Hardwood & Shredded Pine Bark) – THE BEST OF BOTH WORLDS, AND THEN SOME. Mixed Mulches also have the ability, because of the pine bark mulch, to prevent the onset of saprophytic ooze discussed in the shredded hardwood variety. This variety is mostly found in bulk at soil yards and not labeled as such in bags. It can also cost a bit more, even in bulk, than the basic shredded varieties of hardwood and pine bark.

**Black Diamond** (Another blend of Shredded Hardwood & Shredded Pine Bark – But Darker) -- However, Black Diamond is a very specifically marketed version of mixed mulch. It comes from the parent company, Living Earth Technology (LETCO), but they make a different signature line of mulches and amendments called Earth's Finest. That's the label that specifically carries the Black Diamond mulch. Some people have correctly noticed that mixed mulches that come from bags, such as Black Diamond, are darker than the bulk version of mixed mulch. This occurs because the bagged material has "composted" a bit more intensely. I've never found a natural mulch that holds its color longer than Black Diamond. Dyed mulches may stay darker longer, but they don't come by it naturally.

**Living Mulch** (Shredded Hardwood and Compost) – This is relatively new to the Gulf Coast market, but it may be one of the ultimate 2-for-1 bets to come around. Think about it: We need compost to build beds with, and we need our mulches to break down and be part of the beds eventually. I can think of no other way of accelerating the process than by blending the two. Viola! I give you Living Mulch – a perfect blend of compost and shredded hardwood mulches. As of 2005, I am aware of only one company that makes this, and that just happens to be the company that pretty much set the standards for Organic Gardening in Texas -- Garden-Ville. But watch, because 10 years ago very few companies had shredded hardwood mulches in the pipeline. Now everyone has one.

**Leaves & Grass Clippings** – If you produce a lot of grass clippings from a bagging-type mower and if you have a lot of leaves from trees on your property, you can basically make your own mulch with a combination of the two. However, it is always best to compost them for a few months (six months would be even better), before using them as mulch. Still, if you're pressed for cash and you are overflowed with grass and leaves, then they can make good mulch. Obviously, they will blow away and wash away a bit more easily than any of the previously mentioned mulches. Furthermore, there are certain trees whose leaves you should avoid all together such as, Pecan, Hickory and some Live Oaks. Unless you compost the leaves from those trees, there is a tannin compound in them that taints the soils of shrub, flower and vegetables beds when applied as a mulch. Again, that's why it's so important to break them down into compost for a few months before using them as mulch.

**Pine Needles** – While pine needles are slow to decompose, the flip side to that is that they are incredibly long lasting. I also think they make an awesome mulch for the Yah-Yah plants because they do impart a tiny bit of acid to the soil for those plants who could benefit from it. In fact, they may be one of the more perfect mulches for tree rings, especially pine trees. Plus, a thick layer of pine needles may be the ultimate weed barrier because you can put it down much thicker than the shredded mulches. As such, I don't know many weeds that try to germinate through such a uniquely intertwined matting of pine needles. Thus, the downside to pine needles is that unless it's for use specifically on some of the Yah-Yah plants or trees, you really don't want to add that much acid over time to plants that need a more neutral environment. Lastly, it's important to note on the downside, that pine needles are not always that readily available in retail settings. However, if you have a lot of pine trees already, you have a free source.

**Shredded Red Cedar** – Much like the other shredded varieties of wood mulches, shredded red cedar will stay in place longer. The three benefits of shredded red cedar are its color, aroma when first applied and natural insect repellency. The downsides are that it cost much more than any of the other shredded wood versions, it's not the insect repellant panacea that some would have you believe (I'll have to tell you about the story of a fire ant mound that built itself in half of an open bag of my cedar product a few years ago.) and you have to really like or want that red color in your beds. That's obviously a personal aesthetics questions that only you can answer.

**Shredded Cypress Mulch** – Take much of what we just discussed about shredded red cedar and apply it to shredded cypress mulch. It's more expensive that the average mulch, looks different in color, has a natural insect and reptile repellency and has a uniquely pleasant aroma when first applied.

**Composted Humus** -- Let's first assume you have a compost pile. Well, then you can compost all those leaves and grass clippings into a free source of instant mulch. While the upside is that it's free mulch – if you will – the down side is that weeds love to set up shop in rich, organic compost. To me, there is a sort of a simple irony when developing composted humus. Along the Gulf Coast, if you want to block weeds, you still have to put some kind of barrier mulch on top. Still, by organic gardening standards, composted humus is bona fide mulch.

What are my favorite mulches? I prefer the mixed mulch and the Black Diamond style of mulches because of the aesthetics, but they certainly aren't always as cost effective as shredded hardwood and/or shredded pine bark. I will say that if I could only choose one and one only to meet my aesthetics and be the most cost effective, I would have to opt for the mixed mulch or Black Diamond any day of the week. However, the recent introduction of living mulches may soon change all of that. But, as of the writing of this book, the product is relatively new and not necessarily thoroughly tested or known to even be available to the masses in a retail venue.

There are many other forms of mulch out there and even some man-made ones, such as those made out of recycled tires or recycled newspapers. In my opinion, most of them don't really fall into the "landscaping" mode and probably should be avoided. Of course, if you're just downright adventuresome, then you might consider these other alternatives:

Synthetic rubber products from old tires.

Processed cellulose material (from old newspapers).

Pine bark nuggets.

Shredded newspaper.

Crushed rock/granite/haydite

(Not a bad idea for Xeriscaping).

Landscape fabric.

Hay straw.

Kiln fired rocks.

Many of you may be asking about the advent of dyed mulches. Personally, I would never use them in my garden. I understand they are supposed to "keep their color" for a lot longer than many natural mulches, but they just don't break down into organic matter in the garden fast enough for me. Besides weed suppression, I think the organic breakdown is a true hidden advantage. It's also no secret that when you want to add elements (like seasonal color) to a bed with dyed mulch, all the mulch has to be moved completely aside. By contrast, many of the fine shredded varieties don't have to be pushed aside because they benefit the planting hole. To me, the "color" in the dyed mulches is somewhat phony and not natural looking at all. One day they may perfect this process to be more like the shredded varieties of mulches. Until then, I personally would avoid using dyed mulches.

## MULCH RINGS AROUND TREES.

Anyone that knows most of my philosophies on gardening along the Gulf Coast should already be aware that I normally hate the idea of trying to "garden" around the mulch ring of most trees. There are some exceptions, especially with regards to ornamental or accent trees. But, when it comes to big trees, I'm still a firm believer that all they need is a mulch ring around their base. That mulch ring can be two, three, four or even up to five feet on each side, depending on the size of the tree.

Some 30 years ago, most of the mulches we have been discussing weren't readily available and thus, not extensively used in gardening practices along the Gulf Coast. As a result, we no longer have to let grass grow up to the base of the tree. Instead, we can create a mulch ring. Unfortunately, too many people try to "garden" in the mulch ring. However, with the minor exception of groundcover use, I think the mulch rings should be left alone.

The root competition from the big hardwood trees, and even in some cases pine trees, will always win the battle for space, moisture and nutrients. Thus, the attempted flowers or shrubs usually wither away. Leaving the mulch ring alone will allow the roots of the tree to breath a little easier and still makes for quite a distinctive look in the landscape.

But, exactly how much mulch you put around the base of the trees is another one of those areas that have gotten me in trouble. My mantra doesn't work here, when I tell people "You can never have enough mulch!" That's because you can have too much mulch in this instance and that's not a good thing for the tree's root system. So, the supposed freestanding mulch ring around most trees should not be more than two to three inches thick.

I realize many of you see what I refer to as "Mulch Volcanoes" around many newly planted trees on model homes all over the Gulf Coast. This is yet another area where I get in trouble with my original philosophy about "You can never have enough mulch." You have to understand that in the case of trees, too much can be a very bad thing. I find the Mulch Volcanoes of model homes very unfortunate in that it encourages the gardening naïve to do the same. I'm telling you right here and now it's entirely unhealthy for the tree. I also promise it is the worst environment in which to plant annuals, despite what you see the model homes doing. Too much mulch around the roots of trees, in general, causes too many of the tree's roots to rise up through that mulch, looking for moisture or just feeling free to move about.

## HOW THICK SHOULD IT BE?

I like my mulch to be no greater than 3 inches in almost all places, but no less than 2 inches as well. But, this is assuming I'm using the kind of mulches that also break down and help amend the soil over time. This thickness applies to flower beds, shrub beds, tree rings and even vegetable gardens.

Yes, there are some caveats to this general practice. Obviously, you don't necessarily need three inches in newly planted veggie gardens, or those areas sown with seed, so that you don't thwart the growth of the baby transplant or struggling seed. The same concept holds true for newly planted annuals that may be relatively small upon planting. Once the vegetables or flowers come to more maturity and size, then you can start adding back to the mulch level to reach three inches. Which, again, is another great reason to have extra bags of mulch handy for just such repair purposes.

At this depth, one cubic yard covers approximately 100 square feet. To figure how much to buy you will need to find the square footage of the area you wish to mulch. Divide that number by 100 and this will be how many cubic yards you need. If you buy it by the bag, you will need at least 13 bags that contain at least two cubic feet in order to make one cubic yard. It would take 9 bags with at least three cubic feet to make one cubic yard.

## DE-MYSTIFYING THE MULCHING MYTHS

You can always bet that when someone tells a consumer that mulches attract termites, they are usually selling something on the other end of the statement. It could be another mulch alternative they're peddling or even a termite control. It's simply not true that mulches attract termites. Yes, termites love cellulose material but they aren't "attracted" to shredded mulches in the first place, and termites are pretty much already there. (THEY'RE EVERYWHERE: Again, that's a chapter in another book for another time.) Bottom Line: Don't let anyone convince you that shredded wood mulches are going to attract termites. They would much prefer the white woods that lumber usually comes from; not decomposing shards of what used to be wood, now mixed with composts, or already decomposing on its own.

That actually leads perfectly into the next point. Some people think compost and mulches attract unwanted insects. Any organic material has the capability of drawing insects or bugs. This is not always bad because it is a part of the natural scheme of things. The mulch will not attract any more bugs or insects than would already be there.

What about repelling bugs with certain mulches? Cedar and cypress mulches have been marketed in recent years as a "natural" pest control/repellant/alternatives. While there has been some anecdotal evidence of these working to deter insects from entering the areas where the mulch is laid, scant empirical research exists to prove these points. I will agree that cedar oils in the cedar-style mulches are a known insect repellant or deterrent. But, since it's the oils that do the work, they have to be released to perform their job; if you are using cedar mulches to be your insect control you have to go scratch the top of the mulch to release the oils. I'm not certain that anyone is going to do that every other day for "natural" insect repellency.

"There's an ooze in my mulch!" I get that question/statement quite a bit on my radio program, and have answered literally hundreds of emails on that very subject. First, let me say I've heard it described many ways:

"An ooze coming from my mulch."
"Something that looks like wet scrambled eggs."
"I think my cat regurgitated his breakfast in my garden."
"I swear it's as if a dog has thrown up in my mulch."

It is technically labeled as:

Scrambled Egg Slime Mold
Saprophytic Fungus
or, just plain Slime Mold.

If you deal with shredded hardwood mulch in a landscape, sooner or later you're going to have an incidence of saprophytic fungus/slime mold. It normally starts as a wet-yellow or wet-orange blob on the top of a mulched bed. Then, in most cases, it hardens and turns tan and finally becomes a brownish pile of dust. While the wet stage only lasts 24-36 hours, the hardened, brown-spore stage can last up to a month.

In 1973, yellow, pulsating blobs of "scrambled egg" slime plasmodia appeared in Dallas and caused a near panic. Some residents thought these "blobs" were either aliens from outer space or mutant bacteria preparing to take over the earth! Typical Dallas-ites! (I can say that without too much retribution because this is supposed to be for Gulf Coast gardeners, right?!?!) While it may seem odd to some, "scrambled egg" slime mold and a similar type are fried and eaten by natives of Veracruz, Mexico. They're called "caca de luna" by the locals. I'm not making this stuff up!!! In the Houston area, it is almost always associated with shredded hardwood mulches. It gets energy from organic matter below the soil line rather than from the sun, like green plants. If a fungus feeds on living organic matter, it is called parasitic. If it feeds on non-living organic matter, it is called saprophytic (pronounced: sah-pro-fit'-ik).

Is it a good thing or a bad thing? I think it's a good thing because it shows high levels of organic matter trying to do something. Can you control it? Do you even need to control it? You can control it simply by flipping it over before it gets to the hardened stage. Anyone who has tried to flip the hardened stage with its countless brown spores knows what an effort in futility that can be. But, if you catch it in that oozy, wet stage, you can flip it over and soak the area with a fungicide like Consan. Once it's dried and hard, forget about spraying it with anything. And, yes, you can just leave it alone.

# Chapter Seven-

# Indoor Houseplants
# Made Easy

If you could ever look in my Virtual Garage (that would be my brain), not only do I have lots of gardening materials cluttering things up, but I also have way too many SOAP BOXES.

There are so many gardening issues that get my proverbial dander up that I could go on about all day. That list of soapbox issues includes the pathetic job supposed landscapers do on new construction homes, mulch-mowing versus bagging and the use of weed-and-feeds with atrizine. But, my biggest soap box issue has got to be this trend toward plastic indoor plants.

First, don't even try to tell me that you have a brown thumb, or that you'll never have a green thumb and that's why you won't try to grow indoor plants. That's the worst excuse for not growing live tropical plants inside the house. I'm a firm believer that if I can grow indoor/tropical plants successfully, anyone can. Although, I will have to admit that it was touch-and-go for awhile after the birth of our son. With his curiosity and willingness to put anything and everything into his mouth, most of my indoor plants were banished to the back porch and their care suffered. Now that my son is old enough, those plants are slowly making their way back indoors.

I freely admit that we have lots of fake plants in the Lemmon household, but in almost every case, they are positioned in hard-to-reach/impossible-to-water places. To me, there's nothing better at adding a comfortable feeling to the home than adding live plants. A ficus tree here and a China doll there and not only is the bare room graced with a living plant, but you have added a soothing effect to the room as well.

Then, of course, there's the list of healthful benefits you get from indoor plants. Plants are able to absorb pollutants from the air, making it cleaner and more pure. Plants are effective in cleaning the indoor air. They absorb toxins (VOCs) emitted by modern buildings, furnishing materials, electronic equipment and even exhaust fumes which may enter buildings through windows and doors. Plants generally make us feel better – 82 percent of those questioned said so in a recent Royal Horticultural Society survey. Low levels of chemicals such as carbon monoxide and formaldehyde can be removed from indoor environments by plant leaves alone

And you too can grow indoor plants, if you follow a few basic rules, turning brown thumbs green in a matter of weeks. As the British would say - they're all "right proper."

1. Proper Soil

2. Proper Drainage & Moisture Retention

3. Proper Lighting Requirements

4. Occasional Feedings (Not very proper, I admit)

5. Proper Plant Selections.

## PROPER SOIL

First, no matter what the situation (You buy one; get one as a gift; are willed one by someone who is moving etc.) immediately change the potting soil. That's because the soil that the plant comes in is usually too light and fluffy. It needs to be that way for the floral shop or nursery because they usually water the plant every single day. You won't.

So, logically you shouldn't buy that kind of fluffy potting soil either -- unless you do want to water every day. That means stop buying the fluffiest potting soil you find on shelves of mass-merchandisers. While this is good if you own a nursery or floral shop, it's too light and drains too fast, thus forcing you to water every day.

The best potting soil is definitely fluffier than outdoor bedding soil, but actually has some soil in it. They also have some sand, haydite or perlite. That way, these soils will hold on to the moisture for longer than a day. There are marketed bags of Organic Potting Soil, Humus Soil and others that I think work fine. My favorites are Lady Bug Natural Brand Vortex Potting Soil, Jungle Growth and Easy Gro Premium Potting Soil.

# PROPER DRAINAGE & MOISTURE RETENTION

Once you have the right kind of potting soil, then you're already heading in the right direction for moisture retention. Improper watering and/or improper drainage is the single biggest reason the average houseplant dies. Over-watering and under-watering are the two biggest culprits. Unless you totally ignore your plants and they dry and die, it's the over-watering that ends up being the most common death sentence. This is because the excess water combines with improper drainage and forces the roots of the plant to rest in water, essentially drowning the roots.

So, how much water should you give your plants? It would be simple to say, once a week. But it's not that simple. Light factors, temperature, humidity and the container combine to alter the water requirements of each plant. Still, there's no need to become a gadget-collector to help you read soil moisture because it simply comes down to using your eyes and your fingers.

Assuming you're using the right soil and have the proper drainage, if your plant is drooping or wilting, chances are it needs a drink of water. However, the sight-method alone doesn't always work. Thus, the most tried and true method of judging a plant's water needs is the finger test. You simply poke your index finger an inch or so into the soil and if it feels dry, add some water. If the soil is still moist to the touch, it doesn't need water. And here's the tough part, you have to test them once every week to two weeks. Yes, I realize that is so arduous. Actually, if you do this consistently, you will have a routine down and instinctively know when the plants need watering. Thus, the finger test will become a thing of the past.

If you're like me, you'll water some plants once every two weeks and some plants once a week because some dry out quicker than others. Besides, it's really easy to establish a routine. When watering plants, it's also important to remember that plants really need a thorough soaking. If you only water the top couple of inches, the roots will never receive an adequate amount of moisture.

That leads us back to the drainage issue. Assuming you have the proper planting mix/soil, you must also create a drainage pattern at the bottom of the container. Horticulturists on television, as well as authors of other gardening books sing the praises of broken pieces of terra cotta clay pots at the bottom to create good drainage. It's an excellent idea. But, what if you don't have any terra cotta pots to break? In lieu of that, you can use broken pieces of brick. I've successfully used pea gravel and river rock. Still others have used broken twigs and large pieces of pine bark nuggets. Any of these items placed at the bottom of every houseplant container allows for proper drainage. Also, don't forget the drainage holes. Most containers have them, however, if by chance they don't, you'll need to create two to three drainage holes on the bottom of the container.

## PROPER LIGHT REQUIREMENTS

I think this is fairly simple to determine. Most house plants grow in areas of lots of indirect light. That means they need lots of light, but no direct sunlight. Think about the atriums of many office buildings. They usually have opaque roofs that let plenty of light in, but, no direct sunshine. If you get early morning sun from east-facing windows, that's usually okay for some tropicals. However, west-entering sun is usually deadly to such plants. If you can't provide consistent, indirect light, then lots of fluorescent lighting will often work.

## OCCASIONAL FEEDINGS

I think this concept is fairly easy, too. The key word is OCCASIONAL. For most houseplants, all it takes is a twice-a-year feeding. I'm not kidding. They make slow-release granules, houseplant spikes and of course, the ever-popular water-soluble fertilizers. As long as you stay away from Bloom Booster types of fertilizers (really high middle numbers like 10-50-10), it seems that almost anything will work. My personal choice is Medina Hasta Gro, a 6-12-6 organically derived all-purpose fertilizer. However, anything that is considered "organic" will also work. Plus, anything with a first number higher than all the others, but still well-balanced will work too – such as 8-2-4; 4-1-2; 4-2-2.

Another great feeding tip for greening up some yellowing indoor plants is fish emulsion. If you can handle the smell, feed the plants once a year outdoors with fish emulsion and you'll see an intense greening up. Better yet, the evolution of the liquid organic fertilizers, as noted above, are starting to incorporate a low-odor version of fish emulsion in some of their newer blends.

## PROPER PLANT SELECTION

I'll just give you my list. I've found that if you follow the rules already discussed and pick any of these plants, you will succeed.

Arrowhead (Syngonium)

Asparagus Fern (Sprenger Fern)

Aspidistra (Cast Iron Plant)

Bromeliads

China Doll

Chinese Evergreens (Aglaonema)

Diffenbachia (Dumb Cane)

Dracaena (Corn Plants)

Ficus Tree (Ficus Benjamina)

Parlor Palm (Kentia Palm)

Philodendron

Pothos Ivy

Rubber Tree Plant (Ficus Elastic)

Schefflera

Snake Plant (Mother-In-Law Tongue)

Spathiphyllum (Peace Lily)

Spider Plant (Airplane Plant)

Tolmiea (Mother of Thousands; Piggyback Plant)

Important things to remember about care of house plants:

- Water in the mornings.
- Water with room temperature water.
- If you're watering every day, you need better soil.
- Don't forget the drainage zone needed at the bottom of the pot.
- Avoid watering house plants with softened water.
- Don't fertilize/feed plants infected with pests or diseases.
- Don't add more fertilizer just because a leaf is brown or yellow.

## FUNGAL GNAT CONTROL ON HOUSE PLANTS

I suppose it is worth mentioning that many people avoid using live houseplants because of the threat of fungal gnats. Those are the tiny black fruit flies that seem to hover around the plant, sink or trash can.

The first instinct for many people is to throw away the houseplant. However, I think they are worth salvaging, and as you'll understand in a moment, the problem isn't always the plant.

Nevertheless, there are usually four places that fungal gnats exist. Yes, they can come in from the outside, but, the only reason they persist is because they breed in one of these four places.

- ☐ Decaying Fruit or Vegetables (hence the fruit fly description).
- ☐ Fungal Pockets in Indoor/Potted Plants.
- ☐ Fungal Pockets in the Sink/Drain.
- ☐ Trash Containers.

So, the first thing you do is look for any of these four situations and take steps to control them. For the first example (DECAYING FRUIT/VEGGIES), you simply remove/throw away the fruit or vegetable in question. They are usually breeding in the mold on the underside of said fruit/veggie that is rotting. This is usually the most pervasive and oddly enough easiest to control situation.

The second situation is also very common, but a little more labor-intensive in the control practice. If you can find the obvious plant that they are hovering around and more than likely breeding in, then the control measures can be one of many. You can drench the soil with a liquid B.T. (Bacillus Thuringiensis – organically derived bacterium) which takes care of the larvae in a natural way. You can cover the top of the soil with about 1/4 inch of sharp sand (builder's grade or sand box style) to suffocate the breeding ground. Or, you can take the suspect plant outside and drench the entire root ball with any liquid insecticide approved for houseplants.

The third situation is probably the most difficult control method against fungal gnats. If they are breeding in pockets of fungus in a sink, that usually means they are doing so just under the lip of the sink/drain. More times than not, they are doing so on the sink-side with the garbage disposal.

Thankfully, the garbage disposal side is easier to control than the sink without the garbage disposal. That's because you can purposely clog/fill the sink with soapy water and turn on the garbage disposal and disinfect the area that the fungal gnats are breeding.

Another fun way to control them is to fill the garbage disposal full of ice and again turn on the disposal switch. The pulverization of the ice will tear up the breeding pockets just under the lip of the sink.

The fourth example is pretty obvious. If you have fungal gnats hanging around the trash can, then throw it all away and disinfect the trash can.

If for any reason you still can't seem to find where the source of the fungal gnat is coming from, there is a fun way to bait them and kill them, all in one step.

It's a simple method of using apple cider vinegar and water. Fill a plastic glass (little plastic see through ones are helpful -- you know, those 4-6 ounce party glasses?) half-full with equal parts of apple cider vinegar and water. The fungal gnats love this stuff, but can't get out. They dive-bomb the mixture and kill themselves. This helps you identify the general area of fungal gnat infestation, and more importantly, it helps control them.

# Chapter Eight-

# Philosophical Meanderings

When I first came to Houston (via Texas A&M University's faculty/staff) to do the GardenLine radio program, I never imagined it would be a job that would last for more than a few years. It's been humbling in many ways that it has lasted for a decade. It is even more bizarre when you find out that people will do absolutely whatever you tell them to do as a garden advice guru.

That taught me to have certain philosophies and principles that work as a backbone for solid advice in this business. I would venture to guess that many people who have listened to my program, subscribed to my email tips or read magazine or newsletter articles I have written, know what some of these philosophies or tenets are:

## Don't Expect Mass Merchandisers to Be Much Help!

It may seem that I pick on "Big Box Stores" or "Mass Merchandisers" during my radio program, but I think it's for a very good reason. There's usually never anyone employed there that can answer simple gardening questions or dole out sound advice. While that is all very true, the main reason I have problems with the big box stores is that they don't stock the truly regional products. In fact, very few of the items listed on my fertilization schedule can be found at a mass merchandiser. That's because they have to order for all their stores throughout the U.S. That means that you will always see the nationally marketed brands and not the ones designed for the Gulf Coast.

Let's set the record straight on a couple of things related to box stores. Yes, I go to my big box store all the time and buy really cheap plants. I also go there to get certain fungicides or insecticides that I know they have at cheaper prices. But, for the first-time gardener/the first time homeowner, this is probably the worst place they can go for information.

For the most part there are few, if any, "dedicated" employees to the supposed garden centers of these mass merchandisers. I was at one just the other day, getting some paint, and the young lady who checked us out with our hardware purchases was talking about how she was glad to be inside as opposed to being in the garden center where she was assigned the day before. YIKES! I would have hated to see what kind of advice she had for the first-time gardener.

Then there's the ultimate "test" you can pull on someone at a mass merchandising garden center. Ask them what you can use to get rid of Poison Ivy. They will tell you Roundup in almost every case. Roundup is a great glyphosate herbicide, which is specifically a weed and grass killer. Poison Ivy is considered a woody vine. It needs a brush killer herbicide to really knock it out. If you ask what fertilizer to use, and they push a weed and feed formula, you know they don't understand gardening advice for the Gulf Coast.

**Bottom Line**: If you know what you're doing and know exactly what you need, big box stores are a great place for super values on products and plants. If you are just getting started in gardening and you really need sound advice, you need an independent nursery or garden center. Such garden centers usually have professionals on staff to answer your questions and dole out proper advice for the Gulf Coast.

## It's Never Too Late To Do the Right Thing!

Of course, this is not an "absolute". But, this is a great philosophy that can guide you in your decision to apply fertilizers, mulches, fungicides, insecticides and herbicides. If you'll remember the phrase "It's never too late to do the right thing" it will help you in almost any application of any product.

Here's a great example: Let's say it's May 1st and you didn't do the April fertilizer application as instructed in my fertilization schedule. Do you still put down the slow-release 3-1-2/4-1-2 ratio fertilizer? Absolutely! That's because it's never too late to do the right thing.

Of course, if you wait too late for anything, you may not get the ultimate results. The best example of that would be with pre-emergent herbicides. If you forget to apply the October/November application, and wait until December or January, then you will obviously end up with a number of weeds, because you didn't time it just right. But, even by applying the pre-emergent you still get some weed germination blockage.

**Bottom Line**: It's never too late to do the right thing. It's a pretty simple philosophy and it will benefit you and your landscape to incorporate it into your thought processes when you think you missed a fertilizer, fungicide, mulch, herbicide or insecticide application.

## You Don't Have to Feed Your Garden Every Two Weeks to Look Good!

There are so many advancements in fertilizer technology today. 20 years ago it was common practice to use water-soluble plant foods every two weeks to keep flower beds looking good. Thanks to the development of a number of slow-release blooming plant foods, you only have to feed flowering plants once every three to four months. That means if you have flower beds and change out the color per the season, you really only have to feed them once per color transplant, since most "seasons" last about 3 months.

While I don't know anyone who feeds their lawn every two weeks, there are scores of lawn fertilization services that find ways to treat your lawn once a month. Plus, nationally marketed fertilizers boast the need to fertilize 6-8 times a year. My slow-release schedule, as dominated by slow-release formulas, only calls for 3 or 4 fertilizations in year.

**Bottom Line**: Unless you just really like to foliar feed your flowers every two weeks, it is not necessary to use water-soluble plant foods every two weeks. Just look for slow-release blooming plant foods such as Nelson's Color Star. When it comes to lawn care, there is no reason whatsoever (other than padding the pockets of the applicator) that any fertilization program requires someone to apply more than 4 fertilizations per year.

# Beware The Sunday Supplements for Gardening Goodies!

We've all seen them at one time or another – gardening advertisements in the back of Sunday Supplement Magazines of weekend newspapers. Don't those promises sound too good to be true? - A tomato tree that will produce year-round, trees that will grow 10 feet each year and a fruit cocktail tree that grows more than one kind of fruit. Then there's my personal favorite – Zoysia grass plugs that stay green year-round and will take hold with only a few plugs.

I can always tell when those ads have hit the newspapers, because I get inundated with emails and phone calls regarding the advertisement for things like Zoysia. In almost every case the caller says *"It sounds too good to be true!"*

Well, you know what they say about something that sounds too good to be true? It usually is! First, Zoysia is a great grass for the Gulf Coast, but it must be solid sodded for success. I like the grass, especially since it is more drought tolerant, needs less fertilizer and less water. But, to think that it can fill in a Gulf Coast yard by adding a few plugs, is ludicrous at best.

"Every spring the toilets explode! Every Halloween the trees are filled…," OOPS! That's a line from the movie **Animal House**. How'd that get in there? What I meant to say was, every spring advertisements appear in newspaper and magazines extolling the virtues of plant material and garden products. Some of the advertisements are clearly fraudulent. Their claims are too unbelievable. The truthfulness of other advertisements is more difficult to determine. To help the home gardener, just go by that old standard that I hope your family taught you: If it sounds too good to be true, it probably is. Besides the Zoysia grass plugs or Insta-Lawn ads, here are some others to view with a critical eye:

**Mosquito Repelling Plants**: Citronella oils are natural mosquito repellants, but the oils have to be released from the plant. So, they don't do what they claim by simply planting them in the yard.

**Shade Trees That Grow Ten Feet Per Year:** Yes, there are trees that can grow ten feet in one year, but they are usually Poplar varieties that are nothing but a stick and provide no canopy for shade.

**Fruit Cocktail Trees:** A fruit tree that bears up to three different fruits. Think about it! Even if it were possible in more northern states, our Gulf Coast chill hour requirements would almost always keep one if not all these fruits from bearing. That's because the fruit they hybridized for such trees requires way more chill hours that we can ever get along the Gulf Coast.

**Canada Green:** A turf grass that supposedly stays green year round and can be established by seed. It's a blend of fescues, Kentucky bluegrass and ryes that simply won't work in the heat and humidity along the Gulf Coast.

**Bottom Line:** Just use your common sense. And if it sounds too good to be true, you know it probably is. And if it's garden-related in the Sunday Supplements, then you should probably ignore it altogether.

# Don't Take Part In the Annual Crape Myrtle Massacre!

The Crape Myrtle Massacre is the over-pruning and wrong-season pruning of crapes all over Houston. You've seen over-pruning... people chop back crape myrtles to the knuckles each and every year, and new growth comes out like a "feather duster." And wrong-season pruning would mean pruning them in November and December. Don't let peer pressure by neighbors and commercial gardening crews get to you.

Looking through all the horticultural research I could find, nowhere could I locate anything about trimming crapes in November or December. The reason is simple – we don't have much of a winter. If you trim the crapes in the last two months of the year, and we get a warming trend in January or February, the trees might actually start putting on new growth. That new growth will be incredibly susceptible to freezing weather should it come on the heels of a warm spell. New growth will also tend to draw the cold right into the plant, causing needless damage to a tree that should be resting in dormancy.

Plus, that new growth that feathers out from the so-called knuckles is usually the most susceptible to insects and diseases.

So, say it with me: "The best time to trim crapes is January through February". For years, I've suggested Valentine's Day is a great time to trim them because at that time of the year we're also trimming back our roses. Now, as for how much to trim, it truly is up to you. Since crapes are so resilient, no matter how much or how little you trim isn't all that important. From an aesthetic point of view however, I personally don't like trimming back to the knuckles. But you should at least trim back the expired seedpods (the dried bloom clusters) to insure better blooms in the coming year. You will even find more and more landscapers completely leaving established crape myrtles alone from year to year. They understand that while you get more blooms by trimming old seed heads, you still get plenty of blooms without pruning them at all.

# Organics Versus Synthetics

Does it seem as if you're hearing more about organic-based products lately? You are! Even on my radio show. I suppose the real question is, "Will true organic fertilizers ever gain a foothold in this market?" Right now, along the Gulf Coast, less than 5% of homeowners use organic fertilizers. In places like Dallas, that number is considerably larger (more like 10%). However, it is interesting to note that while the organics market has grown considerably in places like Dallas, the synthetic market hasn't correspondingly dwindled.

This proves to me that there's actually room for both camps in this discussion. Those companies that sell organically-based products have always said that many Gulf Coast communities are BLACK HOLES for organic products. Their belief is that because there are so many petrochemical plants along the Gulf Coast, people are being loyal to the companies that keep the economy flying in these parts. Well, I beg to differ.

The reason I think Organics haven't developed the foot-hold they desire along the Gulf Coast, can be directly related to three reasons. 1. Mass Merchandisers don't carry a full-line of organic products (However, that is changing). 2. Unscrupulous organic merchandisers took advantage of the market, leaving a bad taste in the mouth of consumers. (I'll explain more on that in a moment) 3. Lastly, organic fertilizers themselves have a simple public relations problem. (That too, will be explained)

Which camp do you support? Organics or Synthetics? For the past few years, I've done a consistent job of explaining where I stand on the issue. I still think there should be a balance between the two. I don't like extremism, and I'm not just talking about the hard-core organic person either, because there's extremism on both sides. First, keep in mind that while I dispense a great deal of gardening information to you, I don't consider myself a horticulturist. I'm an Information Specialist, if you will. As such, I do my absolute best to give you information from both sides - warts and all! So, back to the issue about Mass Merchandisers, or Reason Number 1: Organic products are mostly found at very independent nurseries or garden centers – Individually owned, "Mom & Pop" stores.

The problem: The average Joe (or Josephine) on the street, is likely to head to a mass merchandiser first to find anything gardening-related. Thus, their first attempt at anything organic will not be met with good products or good information. Until recently, the mass merchandisers didn't have any focus on organic products. That is changing, but it is a very slow change. One mass merchandiser is trying to set up a centralized, concentrated display of multiple organic products. Still, all that doesn't change the fact that those independent nurseries or garden centers are still usually the better choice for organic alternatives. Remember what I said earlier about new gardeners to the Gulf Coast avoiding the Big Box stores for their first foray into gardening? The same holds true right now for delving into organics. Try the "independents" first. At least there is someone there that can answer your questions.

Then, there's the three-fold PR problem. First, many organic products simply smell bad. Thus, people don't want to open that bag or bottle ever again. That too is changing, and as the technology advances many of these products are finding ways to stay organic but improve the "odor" issue. But the worst of the PR problem is how many companies make claims that the products never live up to. Along those lines, many unscrupulous organic marketers simply took financial advantage of people who were going to purchase anything organic. These snakes purposefully overcharged, hoping to make an even quicker buck. I call this "taking advantage of your environmental fears".

This alludes to that "leaving a bad taste in the mouth of the consumer" issue I mentioned earlier. An example that could still exist today might be a bag of organic fertilizer that retails for $25, and covers only 1500 square feet. Thankfully, more cost-effective brands have entered the market for 15-18 bucks a bag, but cover up to 3500 square feet. I'll let you do the math.

Another reason organics may never take a foot-hold in the market can be directly related to the difficulty the commercial landscape industry has had in "going natural". In an effort to be environmentally friendly, they try an organic program if their customer asks for it. But most consumers/homeowners don't understand the difference in response time. When the "delay" in greening and thickening up is longer than anticipated - a serious drawback to the organic/natural method - the contractor is often left holding the bag. And if given the opportunity to return and correct the situation, rather than losing the business, the contractor generally returns to synthetics.

There's also no argument from me that the synthetic fertilizer industry also has to do a better job of communicating the safety and the benefits of professionally manufactured fertilizers, rather than stewing over the debate of synthetic vs. organic. In fact, most of the fertilizers manufacturers I have worked with over the years, make a good point in their advertising campaigns, that not only do they strive to improve their product each year but "when applied according to label instructions, they will never harm the environment."

That's probably the biggest point that the masses don't seem to understand: Synthetic products are thoroughly tested and their application labels reflect that research. When consumers purposefully misuse, overuse, over apply or simply double the application because they think they have double the problem, that's when synthetic alternatives become an environmental hazard.

In the meantime, as your Personal Gardening Information Specialist (That's almost as long as my former business card at A&M) here are some of the pledges I give you: I promise that if I ever find out that something is truly bad for the environment, I'll be the first person to tell you about it. I will not, however, spread misinformation or twist the truth to bolster one side or the other.

The Dursban Phase-Out is a great example, and a horrible mixed message by the government. They take away Dursban from the homeowners and pest control operators, but they still allow it to be used agriculturally. Do you see the mixed message? The ban came about because tests showed that "over-use" at 500 times the recommended dosage caused developmental abnormalities in baby rats. ENVIRONMENTALIST TRANSLATION: DURSBAN CAUSES BRAIN DAMAGE IN BABIES. See what I mean by "twisting" and "misinformation?"

I promise to introduce to you the latest in synthetic and organic technology in a timely, cost-effective manner. In other words, it not only better do what it claims, but it needs to be cost-effective too. You see, organicides (organic pest repellant alternatives) don't have to be tested by the EPA the way synthetic chemicals do. Remember what I wrote earlier about organic products making all sorts of claims? I bet you didn't know that they don't have to back up those claims with studies, if they are an "organically-based" product.

The fertilizer market along the Gulf Coast is definitely on the move. And several organic manufacturers are building name recognition as legitimate alternatives. This is different from the BLACK HOLE reputation, where organic products would come in and disappear into oblivion.

**Bottom Line:** Just because it says ORGANIC doesn't automatically make it a good thing. If the product is ripping you off financially just to take advantage of your environmental fears, that can't be good. During the past few years, the public has become increasingly concerned with health issues and the protection of our environment, and rightly so. While soil scientists and knowledgeable gardening experts agree that organic matter is a key to gardening success, what they are mostly talking about is additives and amendments to the soil. This does not mean that organic fertilizers are automatically good, nor does it mean synthetic fertilizers are automatically bad.

Finally, if you are suffering from what I refer to as CHEMOPHOBIA (the fear of anything chemical), remember, that you are made up of chemicals, I am made up of chemicals and organic fertilizers are made up of chemicals.

# Chapter Nine-

# Insect and Disease Control

Gardening along the Gulf Coast would be so much simpler if it weren't for the myriad of diseases and the plethora of insects. Because we live along the Gulf Coast, we will always have more insect and disease problems than any part of the United States.

Ask anyone who has recently moved to the Gulf Coast from northern or western states, and they will probably roll their eyes at all the insect and disease controls they have to employ. Have you ever wondered why so many "organic" products come and go at Gulf Coast gardening centers? Our temperate, humid climate is to blame. Plus, winters seldom kill off insect populations as they do in other states.

Speaking of winters, they seldom kill our naturalized and hardier shrubs and perennials, but isn't it interesting that fungal diseases can ravage them? And while our intense summer temperatures can be countered with a good watering program, it is disheartening to see how insects can claim an unattended lawn or garden.

My goal for this chapter is to arm you against the dominant insect and disease pressures of Gulf Coast gardens. The first and most important tip when it comes to controlling bugs and fungal diseases is "DON'T IGNORE THEM!" If you'll just keep your shadow in the garden once every few days you will be able to catch problems in their earliest stages. What I obviously mean by keeping your shadow in the garden is to make an occasional trip amongst the plants.

A former neighbor of mine always complained that I spent too much time in my front gardens. I think he just didn't like the peer pressure of living across the street from me. Nevertheless, I considered my occasional "walk-through" in the garden as much a part of my day as getting the newspaper, checking the mail or taking the dog for a walk. If you make the garden check a part of your "routine" you can pull out simple weeds before they develop a huge root system. You can check for early insects and blast them with water or a simple spray of something organic, as opposed to waiting for a huge population to be "deadly" obvious. If you put your shadow in the garden every other day, your entire landscape will benefit. If you can only do it once a week, that's fine, but never allow your walk-through to become a once-a-month event, or even worse, once every few months.

Insects are very easy to control if you catch them in their very early stages. A cluster of aphids on the tip of a Hibiscus can be blown to smithereens with a simple blast from a garden hose. If you suspect a plant is in the earliest stages of a fungal leaf spot disease, you know to treat it with a fungicide and within days the plant will look normal again. But an insect infestation or fungal disease allowed to linger for weeks can become difficult to control with any kind of spray. What's worse is if you let the insect or disease pressures go too long they can kill the plant.

So, now that you're convinced to make an occasional walk-through as much a part of your daily/weekly routine, let's start learning exactly what to look for.

## MOST COMMON INSECT PROBLEMS IN GULF COAST GARDENS

**APHIDS** – These are soft, almost oval, pinhead sized insects that huddle together on new growth stems, emerging buds and especially on the undersides of leaves. They also come in a myriad of colors. I've seen green, yellow and black ones most of the time. But they also are orange, pink and brown. The most often affected plants are Crape Myrtles, Roses, Hibiscus, Camellias and a host of perennial flowers. If you don't actually notice the first stage of insects, you will know they are doing damage if you start to see a sheen on the leaves. When aphids suck the juices from the plant, they drip a honeydew substance to the leaves below. If you start to see black sooty mold, then the infestation is probably in need of a insecticide control, because it's an indication that the insect has been working for a while.

**Control:** As noted earlier, if aphids are caught early enough (during a walk-through) they can be blasted off with a burst of water. Heavier infestations can be controlled with a number of organic-based sprays from insecticidal soap to Spinosad to Neem Oil. Other "natural" controls include the use of beneficial insects like ladybugs, lacewings and parasitic wasps. The heaviest of infestations need a liquid insecticide like Malathion, Bifenthrin, Permethrin or Acephate. Aphids can be prevented from some flowering plants like Crape Myrtles, by feeding the plant systemic rose foods with Disyston or Imidicloprid products.

**BORERS** -- These burrowing insects love both newly planted trees along with weakened and stressed trees. You know you have borers not only by the holes in the bark or a tree, but by signs of sawdust at the base of the tree. This is one insect that can kill a tree in a matter of weeks, if the borers are allowed to keep girdling the cambian layer of the tree.

**Control**: There is good news and bad news in terms of borer control. The bad news is that the best insecticidal control, Lindane, has been taken off the market. The good news is that the environmentally-conscious Spinosad technology has proven just as effect on many borer insects. But the best biological control for trees, in defending against borers, is to take really good care of the tree. If the tree is never "stressed" or planted in poor soil or damaged, it should be able to defend itself against borers. Again, systemic insecticides are available too, but should be avoided on fruit trees.

**CATERPILLARS** - This is a huge category, whether you're talking about what specifically defoliates trees or ravages vegetable gardens. These are worm-like, soft bodied sometimes hairy, sometimes spiny, almost always green, yellow-green or brown. While caterpillars have a healthy appetite for leaves, they seldom kill any tree or plant just by eating all the leaves. But, remember that many caterpillars can become butterflies or moths, so those that are on flowers and perennials should be left to their own devices. However, the tree-ravaging and tomato plant mauling caterpillars should probably be treated.

**Control:** The best non-chemical control, and the one I would advise using in almost all cases, is a liquid Bt on the leaves of the suspect plant or tree. Bt is Bacillus Thuringiensis, a natural bacterium that targets only worms and caterpillars. When you spray the foliage and a caterpillar eats that foliage, they get sick and die almost immediately. You can also control caterpillars biologically with the use of Diatomaceous Earth (known as D.E. at garden centers) around the base of caterpillar-prone plants. However, if you don't get it down before they climb the tree or plant, D.E. is an effort in futility. Diatomaceous Earth is akin to shards of glass, and when the insect crawls across it, their body is torn up.

**CHINCH BUGS** – This is the bane of most Gulf Coast lawns during the hot, summer months. These tiny black insects have a minute wing pod, which makes it appear as if they have a white spot on each side of its body. They exclusively attack St. Augustine turf grasses during the hottest, driest months. You can rarely see a chinch bug, unless you dig for them or flush them out with water. That flush is the simplest test to determine whether you have chinch bugs. Lay a garden hose on the infected area and let the water run. Chinch Bugs hate moisture and they will run up the hose. There's also the coffee can test where you take an empty coffee can (open at both ends) and push it into the turf and fill it up with water. If you have chinch bugs they will float to the top. Chinch bugs can kill St. Augustine turf, so it is very important to diagnose and treat appropriately. Many people mistake a yellowing turf for iron deficiency or a fungal disease. If there is a mistaken diagnosis, chinch bugs will proliferate.

**Control**: If you want to control chinch bugs biologically, you simply have to keep your lawn well-watered. A well-cared for yard (mowing tall, following the fertilizer schedule and keeping the irrigation up) is the best defense against Chinch Bugs. However, if you diagnose that you have chinch bugs, you should treat several times with a liquid insecticide for best control. Any liquid insecticide will work in most cases. The most commons names in 2005 are Permethrin, Cypermethrin, or Bifenthrin. The trick is in breaking the egg cycle by applying the liquid insecticide every 7 days, up to 3 applications. Most people try to control them with a granular insecticide with just one application, which just doesn't work against these pests.

**FIRE ANTS** – Most of us who have lived along the Gulf Coast have learned to live with them for the most part. Those who are new to the Gulf Coast simply are blown away by them. To know them is to hate them. And if you've ever been bitten by one, you know how aptly named they are. Fire Ants are more reddish-brown in color than the more common farmer ants or even basic carpenter ants. Their mounds will pop up seemingly overnight, especially when the soil is loosened by a recent rain. There is no realistic "eradication" technique for fire ants, since the elimination of Chlordane. Management is the key word when it comes to controlling these pests.

**Control:** Despite the advancements in fire ant control technologies, the most proven method for managing them is known as the Texas Two Step. This is a technique honed by Entomologists at Texas A&M University. There are "once-a-year" controls on the market, and while they work to a certain degree, you still need to think in terms of the two steps required. The Texas A&M Two-Step method requires you to bait or broadcast one control, and individually treat those mounds you see. Unfortunately, most people only do one step. The first step is with any granular bait or specifically designed insecticides such as Bifenthrin, Deltamethrin, Permethrin, Fipronil, Amdro (Methoprene), Logic, Imidicloprid or Spinosad (a true "organic" method). Then search out the mounds or any place that had a mound in the past and treat with a contact kill or any liquid insecticide (organic or not). Examples of these include any liquid Permethrin, liquid Bifenthrin, liquid Malathion, liquid Cypermethrin, Acephate Powders (like Orthene), liquid Spinosads (again, for true "organic" control). The once-a-year treatments you hear more and more about are the Fipronil-based treatments. But don't forget the second step when using such treatments. There is another advancement on the market, and considered the only "dual action" formula of its kind. It's called Extinguish Plus, and it incorporates the Methoprene-based product (such as those you find in Amdro) along with an IGR (Insect Growth Regulator). This could be the best long-term control for fire ants that has come along in a while, but it is still in its earliest stages of results. However, fire ant researchers at Texas A&M have been very complimentary of this new innovation.

**GRUB WORMS** – Grub worms win the "Ugliest Insect" contest in my opinion. This ribbed worm is a grayish-colored body along with a black head. You can almost always find this larval stage of the June Bug (Japanese beetle) in flower beds. It is not a problem until you see 10 or more in a square foot area. However, in lawns it is much harder to diagnose their infestation, and if left to their own devices can devour the root system of a once healthy looking lawn. If you suspect you have grub worm damage in the turf, you need to peel back a one foot square area and look just below the root zone. Again, you would need to see 10 or more in that one foot square area to consider it enough of a problem to treat.

**Control:** Biological control with Milky Spores is becoming more and more acceptable. This is an environmentally safe way to control grubs, especially in lawns. Milky Spore is a disease that specifically targets Japanese beetle grubs and, once in the soil, continues to control them. Milky Spore will not spread in the soil unless grubs are present. The more grubs there are, the faster the disease spreads among them. Imidicloprid-based granules also do a good job of controlling grub worms as does a new product that contains Halofenozide. Another fun way to control grub worms is to actually control the June Bug. Since they are attracted to light, place a white bucket full of water and dish soap (one tablespoon per gallon of water) under the outdoor lamps or security lights. They will dive-bomb the water because of the reflective light, but will be unable to exit thanks to the soap.

**LACE BUGS** – Along the Gulf Coast especially, lace bugs can bring down a stand of azaleas and lantanas in the summer months. Like termites and their inevitability, if you have azaleas, you're eventually going to have lace bugs. They are tiny critters about one-eight of an inch long with a brown torso and transparent, gauze-like wings (hence the name lace bug). They suck the juice from the underside of the leaves, much like an aphid, but instead of leaving honeydew that turns to black sooty mold, lace bugs leave brown almost caramel-ized excrement on the underside of the leaf. In entomological circles this is known as frass. The top side of the leaf gets a mottled, dried-out, splotchy look.

**Control:** Organic controls are a bit different for controlling lace bugs. Nicotine Sulfate has been recommended for years as well as other tobacco-juice-based products. But the three best chemical controls are still Carbaryl, Acephate and Malathion. And systemic controls with Disyston and Imidacloprid are actually the ultimate way to control.

**LEAFMINERS** -- Leafminers are the larval stages of small black and yellow flies (1/10" long), that feed between the upper and lower surfaces of leaves. It's the highly visible tunnels, or mines, in leaves that make most people want to control these insects. All they see is a squiggly line removing all the plants green tissue. Citrus trees are seemingly the most susceptible plant along the Gulf Coast. And if are left undeterred, leafminers can severely restrict the fruit production of a citrus tree.

**Control:** If you catch a leafminer very early, all you have to do is pinch back an obviously tainted leaf. There are also two good organic products for use against leaf miners. One is Neem Oil and the other is Spinosad. When using such organic controls it is always best to remove the most infested leaves anyway, because most of the organic controls work best almost as a deterrent. There are no advised chemical controls for leafminer, since they attack mostly citrus trees, where chemicals pesticides should be avoided.

**LEAFROLLERS** – Much like leafminers are somewhat specific to citrus trees along the Gulf Coast, leafrollers are very specific to Lily Bulbs. More specifically, they love to wrap themselves in Canna Lilies. They are worms that will roll themselves up inside of a Canna leaf and destroy it from within.

**Control:** The good news is that the best control method is also a biological control method. Bt (bacillus thuringiensis) the beneficial bacterium that targets worms and caterpillars is still the best control method for leafrollers. However, it is important to "shuck out" those that are rolled up in a leaf for overall control.

**MEALYBUGS** -- These are oval shaped insects with a white cottony wax on the outer part, which when clumped together gives a look of cotton. They are related to the scale family of insects and tend to group together. They love indoor tropicals and house plants. Like the aphids, mealybugs will secrete honeydew which can give the plant a shiny appearance before leading to black sooty mold.

**Control:** If you can catch mealybugs in their earliest stages of development, a simple swabbing of rubbing alcohol on a cotton swab should do the trick. If the problem has developed beyond a point where a cotton swab treatment seems daunting, try spraying Neem Oil. But it would also help if you added a few drops of orange oil (d-Limonene) to the mix. Since mealybugs love indoor plants mostly, insecticidal sprays are not recommended unless you can move them outside for such spraying, but make sure that the insecticide is not oil like Malathion, which can suffocate tender tropicals.

**SCALE** -- Other than aphids, scale may be the most insidious of insects on plant life. Since scale is circular and doesn't have the kind of legs or wings we associate with things that "bug" us, most people seldom even know if they have scale insects infestations. Scale loves many evergreen shrubs and trees, and even come in forms that are white, gray, maroonish, brown and red. But the vast majority of scale that we see along the Gulf Coast are the perfectly circular, hard-shell dots with the waxy outer coating. Scale loves to sit up and down the spine of most evergreen shrubs they like, as well as the small stems. Shrubs like hollies, hawthorns, yaupons, coppertone loquats and many other evergreens are the main feeding source for scale. The scale that affects trees usually sits aligned on smaller limbs and is often the maroon-brown kind. And like the aphids and mealybugs discussed earlier, scale secretes honeydew which eventually leads to black sooty mold. The best description of scale I heard from someone is that it looks like tiny specs of paint someone spattered over their holly bush.

**Control:** Up to this point, almost every insect problem had a great biological control alternative, but when it comes to scale insects Malathion is still the best control measure on the market.

**SLUGS AND SNAILS** -- Of all the insects I'll describe in this book, slugs and snails probably need no introduction. Everyone knows what a snail looks like, right? The best way to describe a slug is a snail without a shell. They are usually about 1-inch long with a slick, slimy, black to greenish-gray body. In almost all cases slugs and snails feed at night devouring leaves and leaving Swiss cheese-like holes everywhere.

**Control:** There are a couple of fool-proof ways to eliminate slugs and snails as well as a decent biological way, and then there's the "fun" way. The most proven method is with use of the slug and snail baits. Some still have metaldehyde, which was poisonous to dogs and cats, if they ate the bait. But the formulas now are specifically designed to still kill the slugs and snails, while being safe for pets. There are newer snail baits too that contain the active ingredient Iron Sucrate. The most proven biological method is with the use of D.E. (Diatomaceous Earth). But D.E. has to be replaced after a watering or rain. Actually a combination of baits and D.E. is very effective. And then there's the "fun" way, which incorporates the use of beer. Slugs and snails are attracted to the yeast in beer, so people put out pie tins of cheap beer. The pests head straight for the beer, drink up more than a college freshman, bloat up and drown. However, it is important to throw the bloated snails and slugs in the trash, because they can desiccate from the beer and come back to life.

**SOD WEBWORMS** -- These are not nearly as prevalent as chinch bugs are, but if you get an infestation they are just as damaging. Cutworms are actually the larvae of tiny low-flying moths, but it's the larvae-worms that do all the damage. Often times the damage is misdiagnosed as a fungal disease, and thus the populations grow if an insecticide is not used in a timely fashion. The best way to actually diagnose sod webworms is to look for tiny moths hovering above the turf early in the mornings. You may also notice tiny webs in small patches of the grass early in the morning too, when the morning dew accentuates it. These webs are actually spun by the worms and not the moths hovering above. Their name is quite appropriate considering that they cut off the young tender growth of plants at the ground level

**Control**: Of all the insects discussed so far, these may be the easiest to control, since all you need is a granular insecticide. Anything from Bifenthrin, Fipronil, Lamba-Cylothrin to Deltamethrin will work. Liquid versions will work too, but since the worms are likely to make contact with the granular versions, this makes it more cost-effective.

**SOUTHERN PINE BARK BEETLES** – These are tiny little beetles not larger than a grain of rice that creates little intrusion holes in pine trees. Most of the damage is done at about four to 10 feet high on the trunk of the pine tree. One of the first ways to determine whether you have pine bark beetles is the indication of sawdust at the base of the tree trunk. They are extremely attracted to weakened or stressed trees. Another indication is the browning, rusty look to the pine needles. Unfortunately, if the pine needles are more than 50 percent brownish-red, then the tree may be unsalvageable.

**Control**: Again, once a tree is heavily infested, by indications of the pine needles, it should be removed. And since they took the borer control Lindane off the market, prevention is the key to keeping pine bark beetles at bay. If caught early enough, any number of liquid insecticides, including permethrin and bifenthrin, can knock out early infestations. Biological controls containing Spinosad have also shown positive results, again if caught early enough. The best way to prevent pine bark beetles is first to keep the tree healthy, since they attack only weakened or stressed trees. There are also systemic controls with Imidacloprid that can be injected into the tree. But if there is already an infestation, systemic controls will not work.

**SPIDER MITES** – It's interesting to note that spider mites aren't actually spiders, rather relatives of spiders. To the naked eye, spider mites are fairly invisible. When you knock some off on a white piece of paper, you will notice tiny little dots of black, brown and red. But these itsy-bitsy insects can do major damage to Junipers, Cypress, Bonsai and Arborvitaes. They also love perennial flowers like Lantana and Verbena. Damage from spider mites is usually indicated by a browning of growth on the evergreen plants and a washed out, mottled look on the leaves of the perennials. Again, to see the insect, hold a piece of light paper under the leaves and tap. You will notice a scattering of dirt-looking spots, which will actually start moving. If you could see these insects through a microscope they will look like a cross between a tick and a spider. Sometimes, early in the morning a faint web will appear in the morning dew if a plant has an early infestation of spider mites.

**Control**: There are products known as Miticides, such as Kelthane. Even liquid Sevin (Carbaryl products) have an affect on spider mites. But organic controls with Neem Oil have proven somewhat effective against spider mites if used consistently. However, the best control is the dual-action systemics that are Acephate-based (like the product that used to be called Liquid Orthene). A systemic for evergreens, with Imidacloprid, is also a great preventative against spider mites.

**THRIPS** - Thrips, like spider mites, are mostly imperceptible to the naked eye, but their damage to rose blooms and other flowering plants is not. Thrips are tiny, nearly microscopic insects which have piercing mouth parts that can do damage to most any plant. Thrips are small insects, measuring about 1/25 to 1/8 of an inch long. They range in color from clear to white to yellow to brown to black. They love rose buds, hibiscus buds, citrus trees and number of flowering bushes. Interestingly enough, they seem to prefer light-colored flowers such as white, pink and yellow. Dark red buds don't ever seem to suffer from thrips nearly as much.

**Control:** Since they are imbedded in the petals of buds such as roses, contact killing insecticides don't really work all that well once an infestation has occurred. Which is why removing an obviously infected bud is the first technique in managing thrips. You can also take an upper hand in preventing them by treating opening buds with a liquid insecticide like Malathion or Permethrin. Systemic controls with Disyston and Imidicloprid are incorporated in a number of flowering plant foods, and can be another preventive measure, if used consistently.

**WHITEFLIES** – It's only appropriate that this be the last entry in this chapter, considering that Whiteflies may be the hardest of all insects to control, if you don't catch them early enough. As their name depicts, this insect is a tiny version of a white-colored fly with translucent wings. They will fluff up in the air when you make contact with a leaf or branch infested with them. Then, they will settle right back down on the leave to do more damage. Like aphids, white flies suck the life from plants on the underside of leaves, which will show signs with a honeydew sheen first and eventually lead to black sooty mold. Again, if you don't notice them until the black sooty mold stage, it could be difficult to eradicate them, because they have developed such a healthy population.

**Control**: Organic controls are almost an effort in futility against tough infestations of whiteflies, but Lacewings are a known predator and yellow sticky cards have some effect if the population isn't too large. Also, if you catch them extremely early enough, the blast of water from hoses is still somewhat effective. Once you get to the point where insecticides are required, it is important to remember alternating two different insecticides every 5 days. Examples of good insecticides to use in alternating sprays would be Malathion, Acephate, Bifenthrin and Permethrin. For flowering plants prone to whitefly infestation, it is also worth considering the systemic rose foods or systemic azalea and evergreen foods that can impart Disyston or Imidicloprid to the plant's root system.

**Final Note**: Other insects such as **Pillbugs, Sowbugs, Stinkbugs, Earwigs, Scorpions**, **Leaf Cutter Bees** and **Leaf Cutter Ants** can cause damage to certain plants, but only when working in large numbers. Most of the insecticides, both chemical and biological, will control any of these insects. And if you are committed to the "shadow-in-the-garden" concept, you can always catch any of these insects before they ever become a problem.

# DISEASES OF GULF COAST LANDSCAPES

**ANTHRACNOSE** – This disease affects trees mostly along the Gulf Coast. Anthracnose causes large irregular brown blotches and causes premature dropping of leaves in the summer. It can also cause premature twig die-back and canker. And it's that canker that is the source for re-infection of Anthracnose the following spring.

**Control**: The best shot you have at a sort of "permanent" control is to treat the tree when all the new leaves are just starting to emerge. Use any copper-based fungicide like Kocide or any of the numerous banner-based fungicides containing Propiconazol. If you can spray all the baby leaves, they will absorb the fungicide and block any chance of the disease throughout the next 3-6 months.

**BLACKSPOT** – This is mostly a common malady of roses. Blackspot causes tiny black spots on the leaves of roses that eventually turn to a yellow, engulfing the whole leaf and then the leaf will just fall off. If black spot on roses is not controlled at all, the entire plant can defoliate. While blackspot may not be a "death sentence" if left untreated, it will prevent the rose bush from manufacturing its food effectively, and that means the blooms will be severely diminished. If you're going to grow roses along the Gulf Coast, you are going to have black spot. Even old garden or antique roses get a little bit of blackspot, however, they don't need to be treated like hybrid tea and floribunda roses do.

**Control**: Rose aficionados know to spray their roses on a very consistent basis with fungicides. There are so many available, that I'm sure to miss one or two in this list, but here are some that we know work on a weekly basis. (DACONIL, MANCOZEB, KOCIDE, FUNGINEX, PROPICONAZOL (BANNER) and BENOMYL). There are also a number of organic controls that contain garlic and baking soda. But they too have to be applied every week for optimum control. The other way to prevent black spot along the Gulf Coast is to provide for maximum aeration, and remove any leaf debris around the base of the roses. Finally, remember to water the soil only and not the leaves of the rose to reduce the impact of black spot as well.

**BLACK SOOTY MOLD** -- This is not necessarily a disease, but I put it in this section anyway because most people mistake it for a fungal disease. If you have black sooty mold (BSM) you have an insect problem that needs to be taken care of first and foremost. Black sooty mold can be rubbed off a plant's leaf, and if that is the case, then look on the underside of the leaves for the damaging insect. (See Insect controls for Aphids, Scale and Mealybugs) Once you control the insect problem then you can get rid of black sooty mold.

**Control:** If you have in fact controlled the insect problem, you can actually leave the black sooty mold alone, and the leaves will probably fall of the plant naturally. However, it is healthier for the plant to have the BSM removed. There are two ways to do this. You can spray the leaves with a soapy water solution from a pump up sprayer at the rate of 1 tablespoon of dish soap per gallon of water. This breaks up the BSM and you will then need to come back and rinse off the soapy water solution with straight water within two hours of treatment. This technique will probably require up to three sprayings. You can also break up the BSM with a solution of Consan Triple Action 20. It is also advised to try and rinse off the Consan-treated BSM with plain water as well. Just don't wait several hours to rinse, because it becomes more difficult to rinse off the soapy film layer.

**BROWNPATCH** -- Ugh! Brownpatch (*Rhizoctonia solani*) is the worst problem in most Gulf Coast area turf grasses – especially St. Augustine. Brownpatch forms circular patches of brown to yellow discoloration that grows larger and larger if left untreated. This problem usually happens when an unholy alliance of moisture, cool night time temperatures and fertilizers blend together. The night time lows between 60-68 degrees are probably the biggest culprit, along with any night time moisture. You may notice that areas that don't have proper drainage are the first spots to show signs of Brownpatch. While Brownpatch seldom "kills" a lawn, it can leave diminished patches of turf that struggle to fill back in.

**Control:** The best control for Brownpatch is to have a healthy lawn, following the fertilization schedule and watering early in the morning hours. Proper drainage is also a big key to control, as you will notice that low-lying areas are usually the first place to show signs of Brownpatch after cool night time temperatures. There are many preventative fungicides on the market including Banner-based Propiconazol, Myclobutanil, Terrachlor/PCNB and even Mancozeb. Therefore also contact fungicides like Daconil, Consan and liquid Banner-based fungicides. Using the preventative fungicides mentioned above are only successful if used at the right time, and then you have to apply them at least every month once you start such a preventative schedule. Use the contact fungicides in between the preventative fungicides wherever you see a small flair-up of Brownpatch.

**FIRE BLIGHT** -- This is actually the most appropriately named disease, because it gives many leaves burnt-looking appearances, as if someone took a flame thrower to the outer reaches of the tree. Fire blight is technically a bacteria problem that is hard to control because it can be transmitted by birds, insects, pruning shears and even rain. Fruiting trees and ornamental pear trees are the most highly susceptible to fire blight.

**Control:** Considering that this is a bacteria problem, fungicides are usually an effort in futility on these trees. There are two noted bacteria-cides on the market. One is the active ingredient Streptomycin and the other is Consan Triple Action 20. Once you have or see infected branches, they need to be pruned, but with sterilized pruning sheers. You can make a sterilization dip with bleach and water (10 parts water to 1 part bleach) or a solution of Consan Triple Action 20. Throw away infected leaves and limbs, because they are no good for a compost pile. The best time to prevent Fire Blight on ornamental trees is to treat the entire tree when all the leaves are beginning to roll out in early spring. That is the best time to use the Streptomycin-based products like Fertilome Fire Blight Control. The Consan control is usually applied once you start pruning off effected limbs. It also helps to avoid using high nitrogen lawn foods or tree foods around the base of susceptible trees. The rapid green growth can make the tree vulnerable to the bacteria.

**FUNGAL LEAF SPOT** – There are a number of *Entomosporium* fungal diseases of which these are affiliated with. The perfect example of this disease is on evergreen shrubs like Red Tips, Ligustrums and Hawthorns. This disease is also related to the black spot found on roses. Fungal Leaf Spot starts as small brown to black spots that eventually turn the entire leaf yellow. If left untreated, fungal leaf spot, can defoliate and entire hedge row. It's not necessarily life-threatening, but it can make shrubs look horrible if they go untreated.

**Control:** The best control ever devised for *Entomosporium* is Mancozeb. Other fungicides that provide some assistance are Kocide and any Banner-based fungicide. Daconil has been known to be written for this disease, but it rarely provides the kind of control that makes gardeners feel successful.

**POWDERY MILDEW** -- If you have Crape Myrtles or Roses, you've probably had White Powdery Mildew at one time or another if you live along the Gulf Coast. The name is perfectly descriptive, because it is a white powder-looking mold that coats newly formed leaves on plants. This powdery mildew stunts the growth of the plant and can, if left alone, kill a plant in the worst case scenario. If you have powdery mildew, the first thing to look at is how you can improve the air circulation. There are supposedly mildew resistant varieties on the market, but I've found that even those can get this mildew if the air circulation is poor enough.

**Control**: Spraying it once is never enough! That means it can take multiple applications of fungicides to keep powdery mildew under control. Consan Triple Action 20 is very safe for Roses and Crapes, and while it seemingly washes it away, it could rear its head again in 48 to 72 hours. Systemic fungicides like Propiconazol will work a little better at long term control. And biological controls like Neem Oil have proven very effective, but they too have to be sprayed almost weekly until you feel that control is well in hand.

**RUST** – You know that old saying, "If it looks like a duck, walks like a duck and quacks like a duck…?" Apply that to the fungal disease known as Rust. We all know what rust on iron looks like, don't we? Well, if it looks like rust, and feels like rust and spreads on your fingers like rust, then it probably is rust. Rust affects many flowering plants like lilies, irises and roses. It is also a notorious disease on our beloved azaleas. While there are many controls for rust, you can also help to diminish its ability by removing leaf and twig debris from under susceptible plants. Sadly though, wind and insects help to spread the disease, which makes control seem futile.

**Control:** Like powdery mildew, advances with Neem Oil have proven very effective at controlling rust, if you catch it early enough. Fungicides like Propiconazol (any banner-based control) and Funginex are also proven chemical controls against rust.

**TAKE-ALL PATCH** -- Just as it was appropriate that Whiteflies ended the Insect section, so it is that Take All Patch is proving to be the toughest of all diseases for St. Augustine lawns. Whether Take All Patch is a relatively new phenomenon or not is up for debate, but I distinctly remember 10 years ago, very few turf experts acknowledging the existent of TAP. The sad truth about TAP is that most people don't even know that they have it until it is too far gone. When the disease is active, the first symptom is often a yellowing of the leaves and a darkening of roots. The area of discolored and dying leaves may be circular to irregular in shape, which is truly what separates it from Brownpatch to be sure. Then, there is a thinning of the turfgrass within the affected area, and underneath the roots, nodes and stolon become infected and the grass declines. The roots are sometimes so rotted that damaged stolons are easily pulled from the ground. And where the roots used to be are club-like nodes. It's also very confusing through research articles just exactly "how" a yard gets TAP. When conditions are favorable (cool, moist weather), the fungus grows on the surface of roots, stolons, rhizomes, crown and leaf sheaths of the grass and then penetrates and infects the tissues. Oddly enough, as the weather becomes warmer and dryer, the infected plants are stressed, and symptoms become more evident.

**Control:** Controlling Take-All Patch (*Gaeumannomyces graminis*) is not easy and much has yet to be learned about this disease. If the disease is too far gone, fungicides seldom work. Myclobutanil and Propiconazol fungicides have shown promising results. In fact, using those two fungicides together is the best technique. Use granular Myclobutanil products like Fertilome F-Stop or Nitro Phos Eagle Fungicide. Then use the liquid-based Propiconazol products on top of the granular. The down-side to using too much fungicide is that you are killing off any beneficial microbes in the soil. There are even newer methods of control utilizing beneficial bacterium. One such program is called the SLAP Program, exclusive to Southwest Fertilizer in Houston. (www.southwestfertilizer.com) Since the program is in its infancy, as of the writing of this book, it is hard to gauge whether it is truly successful yet. SLAP is an abbreviation for the four beneficial bacterium they use in their program. (Bacillus subtilis, B. licheniformis, B. amyloloquefaciens, and B. parabevis). Programs like SLAP are also used in conjunction with mostly organic lawn care practices for best results. Things you can do to help reduce the possibility of TAP – Don't over water/irrigate, since excessive moisture favors development; prevent thatch build up and accumulation; keep the soil aerated once a year, add a layer of true compost once a year One final note on TAP, and its control: The fungicide Rubigan is still considered effective against this disease, but in many states you have to have an Applicator's License in order to purchase the product. And it is very expensive.

# Chapter Ten-

## Month-to-Month Checklist

There are many jokes about why people don't give out information because you might be on a "Need to Know" basis. And when I wrote this part of the book, my mindset is always, What Do You Need to Know going into each month. The beauty of these lists is that you don't need to commit any of it to memory. Rather, just refer to it once a month, so you know what truly has to be done for that month.

I used to tell people when selling my first book, that this is the "best" part of the book, because it was "easy access" information. The idea is, at the first of each month, or even at the end of the previous month, refer to the list to help jog your memory as to what things can and should be done.

So, now that you are the proud owner of this Gulf Coast Gardening book, by yours truly, you are now on a NEED TO KNOW basis. And here's what you need to know on the ensuing pages...

## JANUARY CHECKLIST

- You should plant tulip, hyacinth and crocus bulbs (those that need refrigeration) all through the month of January. Also, plant any other bulbs that didn't get planted in October & November.

- PLANT TREES! (Unless it is really cold) The third Friday in January is an often used as a regional Arbor Day. It's okay to plant trees that are containerized in the winter months along the Gulf Coast

- Prune established trees in the winter months too. It is easier on the tree to do major pruning during the highest state of dormancy, which is January through February.

- Prepare soil/beds for upcoming vegetable gardens later in the spring. It really helps to let the soil mellow for 30-60 days before planting transplants or growing seeds.

- Incorporate organic compost into a vegetable bed at 2 to 3 inches per 100 sq. ft.

- Check Junipers and other narrow-leaf evergreens for bagworms, spider mites and webworms. Although the plant is dormant, insects can still proliferate.

- Extend the life of Poinsettias from Christmas by keeping the soil moist and keeping them away from drafts and heat. They thrive in temperatures between 60 and 75 degrees.

- Feed your cool season annuals, like pansies and cyclamen. A light application of a slow-release blooming plant food like

Nelson Color Star will be enough until they need to come out in the spring.

- You can start fertilizing established trees and shrubs. You can use balanced synthetic fertilizers on well-established trees (ex: 13-13-13). But you should use organic fertilizers only on newly planted trees (anything less than 2 years old in the landscape.) If you are unfamiliar with the concept of Deep Root Feeding, please refer to the Trees chapter.

- Control scale insect on numerous evergreen shrubs like Hollies and Hawthorns. During winter, you can control them organically with Dormant Oil Spray. Malathion is still the best synthetic control for scale throughout the year – even January.

- Prune fruit trees. Research information on the internet or in specific books, but the vast majority of fruit trees, from stone fruit to citrus fruit, require pruning in the winter.

- Take in your lawnmower and other power equipment for maintenance or needed repairs. Do it now and avoid the rush that overwhelms lawnmower shops in early spring.

# FEBRUARY CHECKLIST

- In an effort to avoid grassy weeds like Crabgrass, later in the spring, put out pre-emergent herbicides right now. You will also need to apply again in May.

- You can prune your Crape Myrtles any time during February. The only "required" pruning is to take off last year's seed pods. Please don't over-prune or prune to the same spot year in and year out. That is what we call the Annual Crape Myrtle Massacre.

- If you have broadleaf weeds, spot treat with broadleaf weed killers. Avoid weed & feed fertilizers with atrizine. The best one for this time of year is Fertilome Weed Free Zone.

- You can provide an early green up (See Turf chapter) on turf grass with a quick acting 15-5-10 like Nitro Phos Imperial.

- Pinch back or "dead head" the winter annuals like pansies and cyclamen one last time, in order to give them one more flush of blooms.

- Valentine's Day is rose pruning time. Prune back hybrid tea and floribunda roses no shorter than 18 inches in height. Make all cuts ½ to ¼ inch above the outward facing buds. DO NOT PRUNE climbing or antique roses, until after their bloom cycle.

- Perfect time to prune most of the stone fruit trees like peaches and plums

- If temperatures are not too cold, you can try a number of color plants that actually enjoy the cooler temperatures of February and March like ageratums, cockscombs, coreopsis, cosmos, nasturtiums, petunias, phlox, salvias, and sweet alyssums.

- Apply Dormant Oil Sprays to scale-prone plants, to help kill any over-wintering insects that might still be around.

- Azaleas will lose some leaves in February to make room for March blooms, so don't panic if you see 10-20 percent of the leaves on the ground.

- DO NOT PRUNE small trees and shrubs that are likely to have blooms. You will be cutting off blooming wood at this time of the year.

- Fertilize Trees and Shrubs if you didn't do anything January. Wait on feeding Azaleas and Camellias until after their blooms season.

- Trim up and shape up ground covers like Asiatic Jasmine. This will help them to spread faster in March and April.

- Start looking for Home & Garden shows to attend so you can get new ideas.

- If you have Pecan Trees, start feeding them now.

- You can start mowing grass for the first time. I suggest you use a bagger to gather up all the debris and dormant grass for the first two to three mowings each year.

- You can still plant containerized trees, if you didn't do so in January.

- Plant the later-blooming bulbs now, such as Amaryllis, Cannas, Gladiolus etc.

## MARCH CHECKLIST

- Feed azaleas and camellias, once they are finished blooming. Then, feed them again in six weeks. If lacebugs have been a problem in the past, feed with systemic azalea foods.

- Prune azaleas after the bloom season as well. Try not to prune more than one-third.

- Fertilize roses once a month from now until the end of September. They are heavy feeders.

- Begin a fungicide regimen for hybrid tea and floribunda roses, if they are prone to black spot. This requires either a weekly or bi-weekly application, depending on the fungicide.

- Good time to replace mulching materials around trees, shrub beds and flower beds, if you haven't done so in February.

- Vegetable gardens should have many of their transplants in ground by now. Don't wait until too far into April. You have to cheat Mother Nature along the Gulf Coast.

- Bag your grass clippings at least once more before mulch-mowing for the rest of the spring and summer.

- Only light pruning should be done on trees, in order to clean up dead or damaged limbs. Remember, major pruning of large limbs is better for the trees in January or February.

- If you've got Pecan trees, and didn't feed them in February, do so now.

- Be on the lookout for pillbug and sowbug infestations. You can use any bifenthrin or sevin-based insecticide, or look specifically for pillbug/sowbug bait.

- You can control the caterpillars/worms that defoliate trees in March/April, by treating all new leaves with a BT (bascillius thuringeinsis) organically-derived control.

- Buy your slow-release lawn fertilizers now, and be ready for application in April.

- Pinch back/prune back established perennials, even after they set their first sprouts.

# APRIL CHECKLIST

- If you're following my lawn fertilization schedule from the TURF CARE chapter, this is the time for the first slow-release 3-1-2/4-1-2 ratio. Do not use weed & feed formulas containing Atrizine.

- Watch newspapers and other publicity for information regarding wildflower trails, and plan to take a trip to enjoy this beautiful natural resource.

- Continue to spray your roses weekly or bi-weekly for control of black spot.

- Plant your spring flowers/annuals now. However, when selecting annual transplants/color flats, choose shorter, more compact ones. The taller they are, the more root bound they are likely to be.

- This is the best month for re-potting overgrown or root-bound house plants/tropicals.

- Move your lawn mower to its highest setting for the rest of the year. And start mulch-mowing until October.

- Plant a tree for National Arbor Day and/or Earth Day, normally in April.

- Good month to start planting grass, now that day time temperatures are rising. This is an even better time to germinate Bermuda grass seed.

- To help control fleas, use insecticides like Bifenthrin and Triazicide in outdoor locations.

- Use Insect Growth Regulators/IGRs inside the house.

- Outside tropical flowering plants, like Hibiscus, Alamanda and Bougainvilleas need tropical plant foods like Hibiscus food. Don't use "bloom boosters."

- Most all flower and shrub transplants do best in flower beds that have been raised a minimum of 6-8 inches above the soil line. 10-12 inches is even better. Use a Rose Soil in almost all cases.

- Although Bluebonnets and other wildflowers look great on the roadsides, they are best planted by seed in October for your own flowerbeds.

- It may be too late to transplant tomato plants by the end of April, but you can choose somewhat larger plants to give you a head start.

## MAY CHECKLIST

- Put down a Pre-Emergent Herbicide, especially the ones that control grassy weeds. Dimension, Barricade or Pendimethlin for the 2-in-1 pre-emergent; Amaze or Betasan for the grassy-weed-only pre-emergent. This prevents weeds like crabgrass in the summer.

- This is the best time to start transplanting the heat loving annuals and perennials like Vincas, Caladiums, Zinnias, Purslane, Moss Rose and Copper Plants.

- This is another good month to replace or replenish mulch, especially if you didn't do it from January through April.

- Continue to feed your roses a monthly application of rose food, since they are heavy feeders.

- Start looking for Powdery Mildew on Crape Myrtles. Fungicides like Kocide, Consan, Mancozeb and any Banner-based fungicide will work. Organically, Neem Oil has shown great results on Powdery Mildew in the past few years.

- If you didn't do the April application of the slow-release 3-1-2/4-1-2 fertilizer (per my schedule), do so now. Remember, "It's never too late to do the right thing."

- Be on the lookout for fungal leaf spots on many shrubs. Photinias, Ligustrums, Hawthorns, Viburnums etc. Fungal leaf spot can be controlled with most systemic fungicides – Banner-based, Kocide, Mancozeb etc.

- Be on the lookout for a myriad of fungal disease on vegetable crops, especially tomatoes. If you see any sign of fungal disease, start and maintain a weekly application of any Daconil-based fungicide (Also known as chlorothalonil).

- Nutgrass can be controlled with one of two specific herbicides, Manage or Image.

- Image herbicide can also help control Virginia Buttonweed, but only if the daytime temperatures do not exceed 90 degrees.

- Best way to control aphids on plants like Crape Myrtles and other flowering plants, is to feed them a Systemic Rose Food.

- Best month to plant large specimen oleanders.

- Don't forget Mother's Day! Potted plants and color-bowls make great gifts.

# JUNE CHECKLIST

- Develop good irrigation practices for your turfgrass. As a general rule, most grasses need an inch or more of water per week, until daytime temperatures start getting above 90 degrees. Then it can use that inch of moisture every few days.

- The best time to water turfgrass is in the early morning hours. Two times you should never water grass in the summer are 1.) 3-7 p.m; there's too much evaporation because of the heat and wind. 2.) 7 p.m. to midnight; get out of that practice or you will be inviting Brownpatch and other fungal disease with that much moisture on the yard all night.

- If you don't already have Hibiscus, this is a great month to plant them, and get instant results. While they love our heat, if you can protect them from the late day sun, they will perform even better.

- Be on the lookout for Chinch Bug damage on turf, especially near driveways and sidewalks. See treatment page in both Turf chapter and Pest & Diseases chapter.

- Remember to feed tropical flowering plants like Hibiscus and Bougainvilleas with tropical plant foods, not bloom-booster plant foods with high middle numbers.

- Make critical notes of your landscape during these hotter summer months. It helps to understand what needs more water than normal, what is growing too fast and how can the landscaping be altered or rearranged.

- Spider mites are serious problems on evergreen conifirs like Juniper and Arborvitaes. You can control them with systemic insecticides like Acephate (used to be Orthene) or Disyston or Kelthane. Newer products with Merit will also work.

- Most shredded wood mulches should be applied or re-applied to help retain valuable soil moisture and continue to block weeds.

- You can do the summer application of the 3-1-2/4-1-2 controlled release fertilizer per the schedule towards the end of June.

- Use of iron/soil acidifier supplements can begin in June. This corrects plants with chlorosis or iron deficiencies, indicated by leaves with green veins but yellow tissue everywhere else.

# JULY CHECKLIST

- Roses can be pruned very lightly to keep them productive and vibrant during the hotter summer months.

- If you're looking for a new annual that is different in size, shape and color then look for Copper Plants or Copper Leaf Plants. They thrive in the heat of July through September.

- How is your watering/irrigation regimen? Remember as the temperatures increase, so should your irrigation schedule.

- If you aren't watering/irrigating early in the morning, start doing so now. Night time watering/irrigation invites fungal diseases.

- Watch for signs of lacebug damage on azaleas, indicated by a mottled, washed out leaf. Treat with systemic insecticides like Acephate, Merit or Disyston. Also, do at least one application of a liquid insecticide, like Bifenthrin, on the undersides of the leaves.

- If you didn't do your slow-release 3-1-2/4-1-2 ratio fertilizer towards the end of June (per the fertilization schedule in the Turf Chapter) then do so NOW! Avoid weed & feed fertilizers at all costs.

- If you're interested in a fall vegetable garden, start preparing the bed now. Refer to chapter on Soils and Building the Perfect Beds.

- You can try to extend the blooming season of Crape Myrtles by pruning off the expiring bloom heads. This can encourage a new -- albeit somewhat smaller – flush of blooms.

- Black Sooty Mold on any evergreen plant, flowering shrub, perennial or tree usually indicates an insect problem. It could be whiteflies, aphids, scale or mealy bugs. Treat for the insect first, then you can wash off the black sooty mold with soapy water or Consan Triple Action 20.

- Hold off on any major pruning of larger trees and shrubs. December through March is considered the best time to perform major pruning. Light pruning of hedge row shrubs is acceptable.

## AUGUST CHECKLIST

- This is the last time you can prune off expiring Crape Myrtle seed pod heads to encourage one last blast of blooms into September.

- Azalea beds may require more irrigation than normal, because the root systems grow so shallow and want to grow laterally, not necessarily deeply.

- Start thinking about building a compost pile. This will accommodate all your fall leaves and grass clippings during the fall.

- Remember to dead-head, or lightly prune many flowering plants to encourage a new flush of blooms.

- It is not too late to plant all those heat loving annuals like caladiums, vincas, celosia, zinnias and marigolds. They will require lots of extra water for the first few weeks, because you're planting them in August, but they will look good up until the first cold spell.

- This is a good time to control nutgrass/nutsedge with a selective herbicide called Manage.

- You can control Fall Webworms -- those that make their appearances in September – by treating the leaves of trees with liquid Bt (bascillius thuringeinsis). It targets only leaf-eating worms and caterpillars.

- If Brownpatch was a problem in your turf last year, be prepared to start a monthly treatment of systemic fungicides as early as August. See Turf Care chapter for available products.

- If you have big Oak Trees with thick canopies, consider having a tree company remove dead limbs and opening up the tree for air circulation, especially during hurricane season.

- If you didn't do your June/July lawn fertilization, please don't do it now because it's too HOT, like 100 degrees. However, you can add an iron supplement if there is a general yellowing to the grass because of all the irrigation.

- Some trees that are under heavy stress, will throw leaves as a defense mechanism.
- Consider deep root feeding/watering of such trees. (See Trees Chapter for details)

- If you're using an irrigation system, always water in the mornings to help prevent any potential fungal disease. Brownpatch spores love lots of moisture on nights where the low temperatures are in the 60s.

# SEPTEMBER CHECKLIST

- The biggest lesson to learn for the many transplants or new residents along the Gulf Coast (I'm talking "people" here) is to understand that September does not mean cooler weather here. If you remember that, it will save you a lot of aggravation.

- Many nurseries and garden centers start having clearance sales. Many sales boast prices up to 75 percent off. It's a good time to stock up on bargain plants, considering that October is reputed to be the best month to plant things.

- This is a big month for fall vegetable gardens. Tomatoes and peppers are easy to grow. Don't wait until the end of the month. They must be protected, however, from potential intense summer-like temperatures.

- This is a good month to plant Chrysanthemums (Garden Mums) from potted plants to the landscape. They will give you immediate color in the autumn months.

- Grub worms can be a problem, eating up the root systems of grass and newly planted flower beds. Try Triazicide as a replacement for Dursban and Diazinon, which are no longer available to the retail market.

- Start building that compost pile with fall leaf accumulation.

- Keep up your monthly Brownpatch control.

- Despite the show of pansies, and other cool season annuals, at garden centers, don't plant them until late October or early November. They will likely die if the soil temperature hasn't cooled enough.

- Consider a fall pruning of hybrid tea and floribunda roses. You don't need to cut as much as you did in February, but more than the ever-so-light pruning of the summer.

## OCTOBER CHECKLIST

- Apply pre-emergent herbicides, especially the 2-in-1 formulas. By applying a pre-emergent now, you block Poa Anna and various broadleaf weeds like clover from popping up in January.

- October is the perfect month to re-do or even start big landscape projects. October is historically the best month for establishing root systems of trees and shrubs before winter comes. By establishing them now, you will be rewarded with vibrant growth in spring.

- It's bulb season. That means keep an eye out for all the bulb marts/shows/sales. Except for the bulbs that require refrigeration, most bulbs can go in the ground any time in October or November.

- This is the perfect month to finally prune those Oleanders.

- Do your Winterizer formulation for turfgrass fertilization. The most important number to remember in winterizers is the last number, the Potassium. It needs to be higher than 10. The nitrogen, the first number, shouldn't ever exceed 18. See fertilization schedule in Turf Care Chapter for details.

- This is also considered the best month for dividing and moving bulbs and perennials, such as Lilies and Iris.

- If you have caladium bulbs and want to save them for next year, dig them up. Store these bulbs in a cool, dry location and make sure all the dirt is off of every part.

- Stop feeding your roses.

- If you like 10-15 onions, and you have a vegetable garden, this is the time to plant them. That's how they got their name, considering that the 15$^{th}$ of October is their optimum planting date.

- Stay on the lookout for Brownpatch outbreaks, and keep up the monthly fungicide control.

# NOVEMBER CHECKLIST

- Now you can plant those pansies and other cool season annuals. Incorporate any of the slow-release blooming plant foods into the planting hole and you won't have to worry about feeding them again for at least three months. (See Annuals chapter for details)

- If you did not do your winterizer fertilizer application, then do so NOW! Remember, it's never too late to do the right thing.

- Cyclamens are the best cool season annual for shady situations. But you can try others like Snapdragons and Dianthus during the early winter months.

- If you know a freeze is on the way, water the landscape plants thoroughly around the root zone. Since the ground never freezes along the Gulf Coast, it is one of the best ways to keep plants safe during colder weather.

- Apply a layer of mulch for winter protection, weed prevention and overall aesthetics. (See chapter on Mulch for details)

- Falling leaves and pine needles make instant mulch for flower beds. There are some leaves that contain tannins that do not make for a good mulch material. Avoid leaves from Pecans, Live Oaks and Hickories as examples of those with too much tannin.

- Don't forget to vote in elections the first Tuesday in November. (That's the most political I can ever get.)

- Consider pinching back (dead-heading) garden mums. They will push out new blooms if you can eliminate most of the expired ones.

- If you have a vegetable garden, consider picking green tomatoes right before any freeze. Fried Green Tomatoes or Chow Chow is a much better alternative than damaged fruit.

- Thanksgiving is considered the best time to start planting daffodils and narcissus.

- Prepare to move Plumerias for forced winter dormancy.

# DECEMBER CHECKLIST

- Find the closest Christmas Tree Farm (www.TexasChristmasTrees.com) or choose-and-cut operation for your Christmas tree this year. It's an experience your kids will love, and you'll be getting a much fresher Christmas tree.

- Gardening gifts are great for the gardening enthusiast at this time of the year. pH meters, hand trowel kits, Bionic Gardening Gloves, bird feeders and gardening books always make great gifts for the "green thumbs" in your family.

- Be on the lookout for Scale insects on hollies and many other evergreen shrubs. Since we aren't out in the garden as much anymore, populations can build up quickly as they go unnoticed for several weeks.

- If you haven't applied that protective layer of mulch in November, do so NOW!

- If there is little rain from Mother Nature in December, don't forget to water the plants and the grass. Soak them both deeply because even though there is little "active" growth on the shrubs and trees, their root systems are still very much in need of moisture.

- You can start thinking about major pruning jobs on large trees and shrubs, but January is an even better month for that kind of work.

- Don't forget there are many other cool season annual options out there besides Pansies – such as Calendula, Sweet Alyssum, Stocks, Dianthus, Snapdragons, Ornamental Kale and Ornamental Cabbage. And, another reminder, Cyclamen are great for shady areas.

- The average annual first freeze date is statistically in early December, so have all your protective work done – mulching, watering, winterizing, transplanting.

- Protect plants from freeze damage with "Frost Covers," sheets and blankets. Don't just use tarps or plastic.

- If you cover things at night, and if the temperatures are above 32 degrees during the day, you need to remove freeze protection, to allow for air and sunshine.

- If you have a vegetable garden, now is the time to plant unusual Cole crops like mustard greens, turnips, leeks and green onions.

- Be on the look out for Amaryllis sales. They also make a great potted gift plant for housewarmings or holiday parties.

- If you need to transplant Azaleas, December is considered one of the best months to actually move them.

- If you get Bonsai plants for holiday gifts, remember to keep them outdoors to grow and indoors to show. They are actual dwarf trees, so they need air and sunshine.

- Get ready to plant the refrigerated bulbs. The last week of December is considered the best month to start planting Tulips, Crocus and Hyacinth.

# I OWE A LOT OF THANKS TO A LOT OF PEOPLE

This book would not be possible without the help of many people, who may not have even known they were helping to produce a book like this. Those people include the many folks who own and operate independent nurseries, as well as fellow garden gurus and even gardening-enthused neighbors.

I will never be able to thank all the people I've learned from over the years, especially from the day I started doing GardenLine radio in Houston. But, I have to first thank John Burrow and Bill Zak for teaching me so many things about this industry, so very quickly. John gets an additional tip of the hat since he was the one that suggested my name to KTRH programmers.

Thanks to all the nursery owner/operators and gardening experts in their specific fields, for passing along your knowledge so I can pass it along to others. Linda Gay at the Mercer Arboretum has been invaluable to me since day one. So has Heidi Sheesley of Treesearch Farms. Heidi has always been there for me. Thanks to Kathy Huber, the Houston Chronicle garden writer, who may not know it, but I read her columns every Saturday before I go on the air. Thanks to Brenda Beust Smith, The Chronicle's Lazy Gardner, for always reminding me "there's got to be an easier way to do this stuff in Houston."

Even more thanks and kudos goes out to the likes of Beverly Welch with the Arbor Gate in Tomball and Jim Maas of Maas Nursery in Seabrook. Not only do they have two of the most unique nurseries for Gulf Coast gardeners, they have always been there to fill-in on the radio show whenever I needed a vacation. Not to mention, they are two of the most knowledgeable Gulf Coast plant experts you can find.

I could never thank all the employees (by name) at Cornelius Nurseries in Houston, but at one time or another I feel like I've talked to all of them. From Eddie to Ken to Kerry to Craig to Steve to Dan to Big John to L.P -- thanks for always letting me come there to pick your collective brains.

Also, a special thanks goes out to Mike James and Bob Patterson at Southwest Fertilizer in Houston. This is the place I go back to each year for a re-certification, if you will, on product knowledge - both organic and synthetic. If I were to open a garden shop, it would be a lot like Southwest Fertilizer.

I have a special debt of gratitude to all the fertilizer experts that intrinsically know so much more than I will ever want to know about fertilization release rates. Dan Snyder of Nitro Phos, Foster Watts of Fertilome and Tom Mensik of Easy Gro - you guys have made my job so much easier, all these years, by always providing background, research and product knowledge.

I'm not a horticulturist by trade, rather an information specialist. But I've been imparted with horticultural knowledge from all these folks and so many others in the industry. I've learned some things (and hopefully, he from me) from my own Uncle Tom (we still call him Uncle Tommy) Lemmon who is in the landscape business. As well as countless other landscapers who allow me run ideas by them from time to time (and vice versa). A great example would be Kerry and Mary Lynch at Buds & Blossoms up in Cypress. I'm not just getting my fresh flowers from him every season, I'm also learning from him how they have evolved from a wholesale flower source to a full service nursery and landscape company to boot. They've kept me in fresh landscape color for nearly 10 years, at a perfect price. However, it's what they have taught me over the years about the quality of good "color" in the garden that has really been the payoff. I assure you, the quality of the flower/color makes a huge difference in your gardening success, not just what it cost.

I also have great neighbors who really "get in" to this gardening stuff, and have listened to all different gardening radio programs for years. They help to keep me on the straight-and-narrow, because they utilize all the methods I talk about. Thanks especially to Steve Jackman, for making it look so effortless to have the greenest yard on the block by following the basics of my fertilization schedule. He is probably my best "trial-and-error" gardening friend. If I get a sample of something, he'll always try it for me. More importantly, he's honest enough to tell me what works and what doesn't.

Another special thanks goes out to my neighbors Kevin Wentzel and Ronne Senick. They had the worst landscape installation I had ever seen, which was installed in August while they were still living in California. They have graciously allowed me to keep chipping away with advice and renovation. But I applaud their patience in this whole process. If I were in Kevin's shoes two years ago, I would have ripped out everything and started over. When I say "everything," I mean the turf and the dirt etc. Kevin's patience is paying dividends two years later. As an aside, Ronne helped with the editing of this book, too. Her payment, for services rendered, was a professionally-planted 45 gallon Laurel Oak.

I have to thank Diane Teas of Teas Nursery in Bellaire. It was her fateful phone call just five months earlier that was the catalyst I needed. She called to ask about getting more copies of my first book, which was completely out of print. After I hung up the phone with her, I literally went to work the next day on what is now Gulf Coast Gardening with Randy Lemmon.

I also need to thank some very important people on the radio side of the business, because without all of them this book really doesn't exist. Sure, I could write a book on gardening for the Gulf Coast, but without the power of Talkradio 950 KPRC behind me, this is just a pamphlet at a garden club. First, I have to give special thanks to Ken Charles, my program director at the radio station who gave me the opportunity of a lifetime just five years ago. When KTRH and KPRC merged, he asked if I would do the program solo.

I also have to thank all the sales people in radio who believed in GardenLine for their potential clients. I take that trust seriously, and most of these sales people know I'll do everything within my power to make sure that their client's advertising pays off. The only trade off is I have to absolutely believe in the product or the service before I will lend my name.

While most of the advertising I do is termed "live endorsements," my voice can be heard of various commercials on any number of our Clear Channel radio stations in Houston. And there are two people that have to be thanked for always making me sound great in those recorded spots. They are also two friends that make it a blast to do production each and every week. Thanks to John "Swifty" Swift and Daryl Cunda, the production gurus at Clear Channel in Houston. By the way, Daryl does the best impression of Milo Hamilton I've ever heard. Also, when it comes to making me sound good, a special thanks goes out to all of my producers over the last 10 years who have had to "put up" with me in the studio -- Tim Collins, **Ramon Robles**, Jason Junker and Troy Bussell. They have all been the ones behind the scenes, creating that seamless effect on the air.

I want to also thank my good friend, and self-promotion guru, Michael Garfield. (a.k.a. The High Tech Texan). His support in all things "marketing" related to this book has been invaluable.

I only have two more people to thank. One is Bob Gunner, who planted the seed (although it took two years from the original planting date) to get me to self-publish. . Finally, thanks to my wife Yvonne, for everything. I wouldn't have enjoyed any of my successes without her inspiration.

# ABOUT THE AUTHOR

Randy Lemmon is the host of Houston's GardenLine radio program, on TalkRadio 950 KPRC. Randy has been doing GardenLine in one capacity or another since 1996, for all three of the now Clear Channel AM stations – KTRH, KBME & KPRC. When Randy took over GardenLine in '96, he replaced long-time Houston radio veteran, and GardenLine originator, Bill Zak. Randy's program is now heard Saturdays and Sundays on TalkRadio 950 KPRC from 8 a.m. to Noon.

Before doing radio in Houston, Randy was the Communications Specialist for the College of Agriculture and Life Sciences at Texas A&M University. Prior to that, Randy served as Assistant Director for Radio and Television Services for the Texas Farm Bureau in Waco.

Although it may appear that Randy has been involved in Agriculture and Horticulture exclusively, he also served as a producer for the R.C. Slocum Coach's Show in the early 90s. And Randy was a sports reporter/anchor for KAMU-TV and KCEN-TV in Waco.

Randy earned a B.S. in Journalism from Texas A&M University in 1984. Then he earned a Master's in Agricultural Education in '95 while working for Texas A&M's College of Agriculture and Life Sciences.

Randy and his wife Yvonne have a 5-year-old son, Randal. They live in Cypress, Texas in a home where Randy definitely dabbles with his own landscape on a daily basis. In fact, the picture on the cover of this book is from Randy's front yard.

# Picture Perfect

## Lawns Begin Here.

## NITRO-PHOS FERTILIZERS

Quality is not taken for granted. We must earn our reputation for quality every day.

**Endorsed by**

*Randy Lemmon*

of the KPRC GardenLine

**IMPERIAL LAWN FERTILIZER** 15-5-10 should be the first application of the year. It contains 2% iron and it works quickly to restore color from Winter dormancy. This 40 lb. red bag covers 6,000 sq. ft.

**SUPERTURF FERTILIZER** 19-4-10 contains advanced slow release nitrogen and 4% iron. This 40 lb. silver bag feeds up to 12 to 14 weeks and covers 7,600 sq. ft.

**FALL SPECIAL FERTILIZER** 8-12-16 is a winterizer rich in phosphate and potash for winter hardiness and disease resistance. This formula provides the nutrients needed by lawn grasses in the fall to ensure vigorous initial growth in the Spring. This 40 lb. brown bag covers 6,000 sq. ft.

**BARRICADE PRE-EMERGENT WEED PREVENTER** will prevent broadleaf weeds and thin grassy weeds all season long. A 10 lb. bag covers 5,000 sq. ft.

**BUG-OUT** contains permethrin on an improved carrier technology. It is an effective control for lawn insect pests. A 10 lb. bag covers 5,000 sq. ft. and a 20 lb. bag covers 10,000 sq. ft.

**TOTAL BROWN PATCH** is a fungicide containing PCNB. This 8 lb. bag is an effective control and a cure for Brown Patch. It covers 1,100 sq. ft.